T

ULTI.

CRUISE PASSENGER'S
GUIDE

to

NORWAY

SamHallBooks

To

Trygve Berge and Annie
With thanks for everything, most especially
your friendship.

About the Author

With nearly 50 years' experience in international journalism and travel, Sam Hall is now retired, having worked with all the major news agencies, including Reuters, for whom he was a foreign correspondent for five years and later their Chief Scandinavian correspondent. He was also an on-screen reporter covering the top international stories of the day for ITN's prestigious flagship programme, *News at Ten*.

Travelling to more than 100 countries around the world, he has covered various wars, riots and disturbances including the Nigerian-Biafran civil war, the Turkish invasion of Cyprus, the Siege of Beirut and the Falklands War.

A compulsive traveller, he walked as a young man from Barcelona to Copenhagen and as a middle-aged one nearly 400 miles across the French-Italian Alps in the footsteps of Hannibal, not to mention another 328 miles from his home in Surrey to Lands' End – an epic journey he describes in his book *'Blisters'*.

He is a widely acclaimed enrichment lecturer with 22 years' experience and has travelled the world with all the major cruise lines. He also sailed across the North Sea in an open Viking boat and travelled thousands of miles in the High Arctic. His book *'The Fourth World: The Heritage and Destruction of the Arctic'* is considered a definitive work on the Arctic for which he was likened in his writing to that of Wilfred Thessiger.

Hall is also a film-maker who, in conjunction with the Norwegian TV and film production companies, Bergefilm and Videomaker Nord, has won several international awards. Many of these films have been shown in more than 50 countries worldwide and ultimately earned him a Lifetime Achievement Award by the British company, CS Media.

Sam is also an accomplished lecturer, presenter and conference host, and an acclaimed hyper-realistic artist. You can find more of his books on his website:

www.samhallbooks.com

Books by Sam Hall

The Fourth World – Life on the Ice
The Fourth World – The Marauders
The Fourth World – Expanding Horizons
The Silver Fjord
The Whaling Conspiracy
Blisters
The Really Easy Student's Guide to Making Money
The Cruise Passenger's Guide to the Fjord People of
Norway

Table of Contents

The Ports

A Nation of Contrasts

Behind every coastline there is, of course, a nation, and in the case of Norway it is a nation that is full of contrasts; of granite mountains and brooding fjords. Of dark forests and glaciers, of wide lakes and wild rivers.

It is a nation whose people revel in their independence and folklore, and yet who are world leaders in industry, space, science and technology.

It is a nation upon which the midnight sun shines in summer, only to leave it in near total darkness for much of the winter. It is, indeed, a nation of contrasts and change.

When Norway was formed between 400 and 500 million years ago, Britain was still part of the continental land mass and when the east coast of Scotland broke away from the mainland, the upheaval created the mountains and fjords that you see along the west coast of Norway today.

There are several reasons why I've called Norway a "Nation of Contrasts".

The first is that although the country is more than 1,100 miles (1800 kms) long, north to south, it is only four miles (or seven kilometres) at its narrowest point.

Indeed, if you pushed a pin into its southernmost point, cut the country out of the map and swung it round, you would find the North Cape positioned as far south as the Pyrenees, Corsica and Belgrade

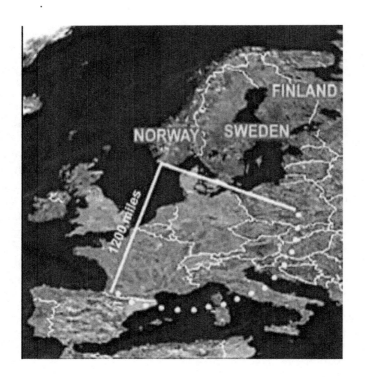

To the east and north, Norway's frontiers with Sweden, Finland and Russia are 1600 miles long (2,700 kilometres), two-thirds of which is the border with Sweden.

Yet, if Norway is long and thin, it nonetheless covers an area of 125,000 square miles.

To put that into context, the United Kingdom, for example, has an area of just 95,000 square miles. But the United Kingdom has a population of nearly 57 million, whereas only four million people live in Norway.

That is 25 acres of land to each person, although most of it is so steep and rocky that it cannot be cultivated.

You might be forgiven for thinking that, tucked away at the top of Europe and separated by vast distances, mountains and fjords, the Norwegians are a somewhat insular people. You would be right!

However, those who live in isolation, in the Nordic region at least, are as informed, and frequently more so, as those who live in other, supposedly more sophisticated countries.

Norwegians publish some 2,500 new book titles every year. In fact, they publish, and buy, more books per capita than any other country in the world except Iceland. They also publish 161 daily newspapers!

In addition, with a thousand miles of mountains and wilderness separating the north of Norway from its capital, it is impossible to over-estimate the significance of radio, television and the internet.

Foreign historians are frequently baffled when a Norwegian tells them that his country only became a kingdom in 1961.

"But what about the Viking chieftain, Harald Fairhair?" the historian asks. "Didn't he unite the country?

"And what about 1814, when the constitution was drawn up? And 1905, when the union with Sweden was dissolved? Surely, Norway was a sovereign state, then?"

"Ah yes", says the Norwegian. "But it wasn't until the 1930s that all parts of the country could receive the radio. "And we didn't get a national television network until 1961. That was what united the country."

In those days, only 5,000 households had television sets. Today, of course television is as much a part of life in Norway as a pot of coffee or a pair of skis. Norwegians today have access to CNN, BBC World, Sky News and a plethora of other programmes just like the rest of us.

Thus, they know as much as anyone about a murder in Manchester, a traffic jam on the M25 or the weather in Pittsburgh, Paris, or Plymouth.

If they wish, they can also live on a 24-hour diet of news, sport and endless garbage just like the rest of us.

In fact, Norwegians are exceptionally well informed. They will discuss everything from the Third World, global warming, Syria and Yemen to immigration, the rights and wrongs of international whaling and fishing, or the sexual habits of a centipede.

That said, they pay less attention to such mundane subjects as the name or, indeed, welfare of their neighbours.

Apart from the super-rich and the desperately poor, 90 per cent of them earn pretty much the same amount of money after tax. They have the same taste in houses, furniture and cars.

They dress alike. They think alike and they go to the same places in Spain and the Canary Islands for their annual vacation year after year. Mostly, though, they prefer to stay in Norway, skiing, walking, climbing mountains, sailing and fishing.

About 12 per cent of the Norwegian population live in the capital Oslo, which one foreign ambassador was unkind enough to describe as "six suburbs in search of a centre".

Today, Oslo is nowhere near as provincial as it used to be and is as cosmopolitan a city as you can find.

Despite the greater city's population of only just over a million people, it boasts some 50 museums, 30 cinemas and several hundred restaurants, and at least a dozen top class theatres, as well as innumerable discos, cafes and nightclubs.

It's a thriving city! Except at weekends! That's when four-fifths of the population leave town, leaving it to tourists and Norwegian holidaymakers.

Most of the Oswegians head for the hills to enjoy 1,300 miles (2,200 kms), of hiking and ski trails that meander through the extensively wooded hills to the west, north and east of the city, just as they do in Bergen, which was the Norwegian capital before Oslo. Some people take to their boats on the fjord. Others stroll in the many parks or congregate around the harbour side.

A few may have to work, but only the dead, dying, drunk or the incapacitated stay at home.

Of course, many Norwegians *are* provincial, which is hardly surprising when so many towns have populations of only three or four thousand people.

With countless communities consisting of just a few hundred people, you might be forgiven for thinking that they are downright parochial, but then for communities in the north, their own capital, Oslo, is 1,000 miles away.

Therefore, can anyone wonder that they view London, Paris, New York and notably Brussels and Strasbourg, the epicentres of the European Union, as being in another world?

In referenda on whether the country should be a member of the European Union, the country folk twice overruled the politicians, bankers and city folk, in 1972 and again in 1995.

They stated quite clearly that they did not want Eurocrats in Brussels and Strasbourg making decisions that would affect their way of life, their livelihoods and their independence. Not to mention their sovereignty.

Yet, despite their fervent independence and geographical isolation, in many fields these provincial, parochial people lead the world!

Norwegian chefs and architects have won major international awards. Norwegian engineers are at the forefront of the space industry.

Tromsø, which lies way above the Arctic Circle, and Longyearbyen on the island of Spitzbergen in the Svalbard archipelago are focal points for the satellite tracking and data downloading industries.

Electronic ear tags from Norway are used to track cattle in Brazil and Argentina.

As for contrasts? We could go on forever.

The Gulf Stream warms the entire coast and keeps even the northernmost ports far above the Arctic Circle free of ice throughout the year. Yet the mountains are capped by several large glaciers, including the largest in mainland Europe.

Half the country lies above the Arctic Circle. Yet, in Tromsø, often described as the Gateway to the Arctic, you can enjoy the sunshine and wear summer clothes in late September.

Meanwhile, no more than an hour's drive inland, the Swedes may be enduring snow and a temperature of minus 10 or 15 degrees Centigrade, or five degrees Fahrenheit.

Summer temperatures everywhere frequently reach 30 degrees centigrade, that's 86° Fahrenheit. What do the Norwegians do?

Many of them head straight for the mountains, and spend their summer holidays skiing!

In Oslo and Bergen in the summer, you can read a book by daylight an hour either side of midnight. The flip side of that coin is that in winter, it is dark for most of the day for several months.

A popular joke is of a man suspected of a crime being stopped by a Norwegian policeman and asked: "Where were you on the night of October 9th to March 15th?"

Almost all Norwegians are fitness fanatics. They regularly spend their weekends hiking, running and skiing through forests, or cycling for hours on a bicycle fixed to the cellar floor, only to rush off to their nearest fast food parlour to grab a pizza or a hamburger with French fries and a teeth-rotting fizzy drink!

Then they smoke a cigarette over a cup of strong coffee, filtered through a lump of sugar held between their teeth.

The greatest contrasts of all are to be found in the topography of the country, the undulating farm and forestland, the mountains and the coastline.

Let us look at each of them in turn. First, the mountains. Here is a country in which more than 40 per cent of the terrain lies above 1500 feet, in which one-fifth of the land is higher than 3000 feet and in which there are whole ranges of mountains more than twice as high as Ben Nevis, the highest mountain in Britain.

Much of the snow that collects on these mountains eventually melts, of course, so we have mile-high waterfalls, spectacular torrents of water that are one of the nation's principal assets.

Some rivers, which can be 350 miles long are so turbulent in their lower reaches that they can defeat even the most experienced canoeists.

There are lakes a hundred miles square, mirrors of peace and tranquility often surrounded by that other great national asset, the forest, and there are fjords that slice through mountains 100 miles or more inland. Think of the effect of all that on communications and transport!

If the people were not to be isolated, the Norwegians had to figure out how to cross fjords and mountains and, to that end, they perfected the art of bridge-building and invented skiing.

They built ferries, a form of public transport as common in Norway as the bus in other countries. Indeed, the local bus is often dependent on the ferry to fulfil its schedule.

The ferries have had another effect on the Norwegians, too. They've made them punctual, because ferry captains are a law unto themselves! Like New York cabbies and London bus drivers, they wait for no-one!

I well remember a stormy night some years ago when a *News at Ten* camera crew and I faced a drive of several hours through pouring rain to reach our hotel. Mindful of the ferry's departure time, the sound technician, who was driving, took all kinds of risks, not least because Norwegian roads are built for Norwegians and tend to be narrow and often devoid of any straight bits.

When we finally reached the ferry stage, we found to our dismay that we had missed the boat. By about fifteen feet.

Despite waving like maniacs and shouting ourselves hoarse, the ferry disappeared most inconsiderately into the night.

Unfortunately, it was the *last* ferry of the night and we were left with no option but to make a detour. Of 120 miles! *That* is why Norwegians in the coastal regions tend to be punctual!

The mountains and fjords forced the Norwegians to learn how to carve roads from cliffs rising thousands of feet sheer out of the water. They learned to drive tunnels through solid granite beneath glaciers and fjords.

Norway's road network includes more than 500 tunnels, among them one that is 14 miles (24 kilometres) long, the fifth longest in the world. Nearly half of these tunnels accommodate vehicles 12 to 14 feet high and almost all the tunnels are illuminated.

With so much melt-water and an average rainfall of four feet eight inches a year, Norway is the only country in Europe to draw its electric power almost exclusively from hydro-electric plants.

There are more than 600 of these and they produce 96.3 per cent of the nation's electric power.

Nowhere else in the world will you find people treating the consumption of electricity so casually. During the six winter months particularly, the lights never go out. Electric heating is kept going at full blast 24 hours a day, every day.

Many is the night I have spent tossing and turning in Norwegian hotel bedrooms, beneath a duvet filled with eider down and with the central heating blasting away like a furnace. Needless to say, there was no thermostat and windows you couldn't open because the local authorities were presumably frightened that you would jump out!

Electricity consumption in Norway is an unbelievable 150,000-kilowatt hours per annum, the second highest per capita in the world after Iceland. That is three times as much as in the rest of Europe!

The mountains and the great outdoors have shaped the national character in many other ways, too, offering the. opportunity not only for mountaineering, but for all manner of sports and, in Norway, the king of sports is skiing.

Indeed, the Norwegians invented skiing, or at least modern skiing. In fact, they had been skiing for thousands of years. Rock carvings discovered near Alta, far north of the Arctic Circle prove that they had learned to ski as early as 4000 BC.

So, it was fitting that these images should be adopted as symbols for the 1994 Winter Olympics in Lillehammer.

Sagas from the Viking era are also filled with references to fair-haired skiers gliding gracefully down mountains and through forests.

Although today our perception of the Vikings is of infamous seafaring warriors pillaging foreign shores, the truth is that most of them stayed at home. For them, skiing was a necessity, not a sport, and so it remained well into the 19th century. Winter snows made travel all but impossible without skis.

Often, they provided the only means of transport and communication. For doctors to attend the sick. For midwives to deliver children. For children to go to school. For farmers to take feed to their cattle or to sell their produce.

These early skis were awkward and heavy, little more than planks of wood, but in the middle of the 20th century, a young boy from a valley called Telemark revolutionised this basic mode of transport and transformed it into a sport. His name was Sondre Nordheim.

He designed a ski that was broader at the front than at the back, and indented at the middle. To this, for the first time, he added a heel binding of willow, which made turning easier and thus gave far greater manoeuvrability.

It was known as Telemark skiing, and suddenly, skiing was fun!

Those were hard times in Norway. Between 1850 and the end of the century, more than half a million Norwegians emigrated to every continent in the world – and they took with them their passion for skiing.

Most Norwegians settled in America. A few headed for the gold rush in the Sierra Mountains where they raced each other on skis 14 feet long straight down the mountainside.

With the winner taking home a purse of 500 U.S. dollars, a small fortune in those days, the gold miners began to wax their skis.

They were the first in the world do so, using wax or dope as they called it, for skiing competitions. Incredibly, they achieved speeds of up to 90 miles an hour, as fast as the top skiers in the downhill event achieve today. The Norwegian emigrants also took with them the sport of ski jumping! This called for immense courage and no small degree of insanity.

Its chief exponent was a diminutive man called Carl Howelsen, who performed throughout North America with Barnum and Bailey's Circus. Known as "The Flying Norseman", he became as famous as the President himself.

Eventually, Howelsen returned home to Norway, and continued to jump until he was 71 years old.

Of course, to the Norwegians, none of this particularly remarkable. For them, skiing and ski jumping, were, and still are, as natural as breathing and it is often said that Norwegian children are virtually born on skis.

Is it surprising then that the Norwegians should have produced so many of the world's great explorers and adventurers?

Take Fritjiof Nansen, for example, whose expedition in 1888 was the first to cross the Greenland Ice Cap! Five years later, he locked his ship, *Fram,* into the ice off eastern Siberia, letting it drift for three years to the Greenland Sea and thus dispelling the myth that there was an ice-free sea around the North Pole.

Then there was Roald Amundsen, the first man to sail through the Northwest Passage and who would later head south to the Antarctic and, on skis, beat Captain Scott to the South Pole.

There were many more: Otto Sverdrup, who discovered most of the islands in the Canadian Arctic ... Ragnar Thorseth and Trygve Berge, the first Norwegians to reach the North Pole, in 1982 ... and Børge Ousland, who became the first human being ever to reach the North Pole completely unaided. Needless to say, he did it on skis. So, the mountains have had a profound impact on the Norwegians, a steady, hard-headed people who, like the mountains, are not infrequently immovable, especially in business!

If, in the mountains, there is a sense of timelessness and tradition, so too with the Norwegians themselves. They have a genuine desire to preserve *anything* that is old and steeped in tradition. There is a museum for every 11-and-a-half thousand people and folklore plays an important role in Norwegian life, often providing a livelihood for country folk dependent on small, cottage industries.

Not least of these is making the 'bunad'. A 'bunad' is what we would call the national costume, although in fact it differs in design from county to county, and often from valley to valley.

Other country folk made a meagre living weaving, creating jewellery from stones and pebbles, glass blowing, pottery and not least fashioning wooden tableware from birch trees, which they felled themselves and dragged through the woodlands to their places of work.

If the mountains were a source of inspiration, the forests have been no less productive, providing materials for housing and shipbuilding. Wooden frame houses, log cabins and ornate stave churches abound throughout the country.

Norway leads the world in the production of office furniture and is a major supplier of timber and timber products to the rest of the world.

The forests also provide a rich source of material for the nation's mythology.

You may find it hard to believe, but even today, there are those who will swear to you that in the very depths of the forest there still live Trolls, those rotund, long-haired, ugly little people with broken teeth and eyes as big as pewter plates, who burst if the sun should shine on them. Allegedly!

But can anyone doubt the influence of the mountains and rivers and forests on the Norwegians? Or the composer, Edvard Grieg? Or Norway's most famous artist, Edvard Munch? Or of mountain granite on the sculptures of Gustav Vigeland?

Centuries ago, the forests grew to the very edge of the fjords, so timber was readily available for boatbuilding.

As the population grew, there was inevitably a shortage of agricultural land, which is not surprising when you consider you consider that even today, only three per cent of Norway's land area is cultivated.

So, some early Norwegian farmers simply decided to move elsewhere and they headed for the coast.

In terms of the Norwegian national lifestyle and the character of its people, the influence of the coast has been equally significant.

In all, Norway has a coastline stretching some 15,000 miles, if you include the fjords and bays, not counting another 35,000 miles of *island* coastline because there are approximately 150,000 islands off the Norwegian coast, the largest of them 800 miles square.

Primitive rock carvings of boats and fish show that the coast has always been occupied.

Indeed, it was because the mountains, forests and fjords made travel so tortuous, that the early Norwegians established their major communities along the coast.

Their skills as boat builders enabled them to cross the oceans while other nations in Africa and Europe, for instance, were still hugging shorelines in vessels that were frail and often little more than canoes and coracles.

In Roman times, the Norwegians were already trading bronze, glass and weapons with countries to the south. By the year 800AD, they had settled peacefully in the Shetland, Orkney and Faroe Islands and from there, they moved on to Scotland, England, the Isle of Man, Ireland and France.

So, the Norwegians of today have twelve centuries of expertise in shipping and shipbuilding! Reaping the harvest of the seas has always been a vital part of the Norwegian economy. Not for nothing is the sea known as the 'nation's larder'.

Whole towns and villages are dependent upon fishing, particularly in the far north, and keeping the Spanish and Portuguese fishing fleets out of their territorial waters was one of the principal reasons why the Norwegians voted 'No' the European Union.

In more than 600 years, they had tasted true independence for only about 80 years and they didn't want to be governed now by un-elected Eurocrats in Brussels. Not surprisingly, the "NO" vote left the nation's pro-European politicians and business executives distraught, but the Norwegians thrived nonetheless, not least thanks to North Sea oil.

That said, they did not squander the profits from the oil revenues, instead ploughing them into state pension funds that are now so overwhelming that all Norwegians are likely to be more than comfortably off for at least another 100 years.

Thanks to their innate fortitude and an ability to adapt, the Norwegians have survived extremely well.

Take for example, the way small Norwegian shipyards scattered along the coast formed themselves into an association that tenders for major orders on their common behalf, and then farms out different aspects of the work to the individual yards.

Whereas one shipyard could not conceivable compete to build, say, a dozen 100,000-ton ships, they are able to do so collectively.

Or take the way in which the Norwegians have developed salmon and trout farming, a dynamic growth industry that now employs 7,000 people directly and upon which 40,000 people are indirectly dependent.

By approaching the industry scientifically, by careful selection of the parent salmon and by meticulous breeding techniques, they have created an industry that puts more than £500 million pounds (more than 900 million U.S. dollars) into the state coffers every year.

Today, the Norwegians are fast developing ways to farm plaice, cod, halibut and other fish whose stocks at sea are diminishing. These so-called 'provincial' people have also built the most northerly offshore oil platform in Europe, north of the 62nd parallel. It is the world's highest concrete platform and the first ever built on one leg, a gigantic mono-tower standing in water as deep as the Eiffel Tower is tall.

Another perfect example of the Norwegian's adaptability is the way in which they have drawn on their mountaineering expertise to maintain the oil platforms at sea. By adapting climbing techniques and equipment for industrial use, they can reach the most inaccessible places in complete safety.

It is known as the Rope Access Technique and it is responsible for major savings in costs. Whereas it took 11 men six days to build and dismantle scaffolding to reach part of an industrial site, a three-man team using the Rope Access Technique did a similar job in just two days.

Yet despite their accomplishments, the Norwegians are not a people to make a fuss or to boast of their affluence.

Today, they have a standard of living that is the envy of most of the world, but they tend to live a low-key life and much prefer not to stand out in the crowd.

The Norwegians are a scrupulously honest people. They are decent, punctual and prudent. They are law-abiding to the point of making you want to scream. They always have a television licence! They always hand in their tax returns on time!

They will invariably have a plastic bag in their pocket when they walk the dog. For years, they would not have even considered crossing the road when the traffic lights showed a little red man, even at three o'clock in the morning when there was no traffic in sight for half a mile!

The country's topography has had a huge influence on the Norwegian's character, the mountains and the sea shaping a steady, dependable people who rarely do anything on impulse! Except possibly sneeze!

People joke that if someone insults a Norwegian on Thursday, it will be Saturday morning at the earliest before they react and probably Sunday evening before they get furious!

Norwegians are a cautious people, too. Trying to get a decision out of them is like trying to squeeze pips out of a ghost. They will sample half a dozen different kinds of cheese and discuss their respective merits for 20 minutes before finally deciding to buy two ounces of Brie! If you think that is an exaggeration, consider that it took thirty years for local authorities in Oslo to decide on a site for a new airport!

Actually, they reached a decision after *20* years, but then they set up a special committee to decide whether they had made the right decision, and it took another ten years to decide that they had done so!

The mountains, the forests and the sea dictate that the Norwegians work, and play, hard. But they live simple, uncluttered, healthy lives and their love of Nature is matched only by their love of Norway.

They are a people whose patriotism and flag-waving are not borne of ultra-rightwing politics or jingoism, but of a genuine pleasure and pride in their country.

Pride in their accomplishments.

Pride in their independence

Pride in their Royal House and in their national flag, and above all, pride in their sportsmen and women. Not that the Norwegians place their heroes and heroines on pedestals.

Hero-worship would conflict directly with their innate sense of reserve, but that, of course, is just another anomaly in this 'Nation of Contrasts'.

***

The Sami Reindeer Herders of Lapland

Sami at Kautokeino.   *Author's photograph*

The Sami reindeer herders of Lapland are fighting a similar battle to preserve their traditions as the Inuit in Greenland.

Theirs is a rearguard action waged against legions of bureaucrats, who appear to detest everything that cannot be categorised and pigeon-holed.

Striving for standardisation, these Nordic administrators provide each new-born baby with a Personal Registration Number.

It follows the child to the grave and must be presented in every dealing with the authorities, with banks, post offices and state liquor stores, or the purchase of season tickets for buses and railways.

It is of little account that such a practice is alien to the semi-nomadic Sami, whose livelihood and culture centres on reindeer herding in Europe's last stretch of uninterrupted wilderness.

Officialdom holds that the Sami cannot be treated differently from other Norwegians, Swedes or Finns. Samiland, perhaps incorrectly, but better known as Lapland stretches across the crown of Europe from the

Kola Peninsula in the Soviet Union, down through the national boundaries of Finland, Sweden and northern Norway to Trondheim on the Norwegian coast.

Approximately 45,000 Sami live in this huge tract of forest, tundra and mountains, the greater part of which lies north of the Arctic Circle.

A 500-mile border fence with watchtowers and barbed wire separates them from nearly 2,000 other Sami, who live on collective farms in the Soviet Union, where reindeer husbandry is a sizeable industry.

Sami from Kautokeino.

The herders have lived in Samiland at least since the time of Christ. They have never sold their land, nor given it away, nor lost it in battle. Yet the Nordic governments, reputed to be the guardians of the world's conscience, have steadfastly refused to recognise Sami nationality.

Legislators carefully avoid any reference to the Sami *people,* preferring to label them the *Sami-speaking* population, a terminology which, though legally safer, is misleading.

Census officials who based their findings on the ability of individuals to speak Sami as a first language have seriously under-estimated Sami numbers, particularly in Norway, where a tradition of contempt and prejudice has forced many Sami to pose as Norwegians, speaking their own language only in the privacy of their homes.

The Sami have been assimilated into the dominant Nordic cultures more easily than the Inuit in Canada and Alaska, because not only the climate is less hostile but also because the Nordic capitals are three times closer to the Sami heartland than Montreal is to the Canadian Arctic, or Seattle and San Francisco are to northern Alaska.

Washed by the warm waters of the Gulf Stream, Norway's coastline, free of ice all year, enabled the Lutheran pastors to travel north easily.

Applying tactics similar to those used in Greenland, they ordered the reindeer herders to burn their drums and banned a popular form of singing known as *joiking*. Those who disobeyed were sometimes burned alive as a warning to others.

The Sami religion was thus quickly suppressed. Later, land taxes were imposed. In Sweden, the government adopted a policy of *containment*, establishing a Lapp zone in which the Sami were allowed to follow their customary way of life, provided that they herded reindeer and did not move outside its boundaries.

In Norway, an active policy of *assimilation* was followed. Settlement in the north was encouraged and rapid.

The Sami in Norway became a minority in their own nation. The victims of outright racism, their children were forbidden to speak their own language at school and the Sami identity, language and colourful national costume became badges of stupidity, best concealed if any form of advancement was to be achieved.

Eager to exploit the natural resources of Samiland, the settlers hewed timber from the extensive forests for the paper and pulp industry, for Scandinavian furniture and Swedish matches.

One of the largest iron ore deposits in the world was discovered at Kiruna, in Swedish Samiland.

The Sami were employed as miners, housed in apartment blocks and given sunray treatment because shift systems prevented underground workers from enjoying the short summer sunlight. To move the ore, a railway was built across the tundra to Narvik, a Norwegian port on the same latitude as Alaska, but free of ice in winter.

As industry expanded, ports, towns, airports, roads and more railways were built. Rivers were dammed, and valleys flooded. Power lines crisscrossed the countryside. Highly paid jobs were created, accelerating Nordic settlement of Samiland.

By 1975, the process of assimilation was so far advanced that Sami delegates, flying to Canada to take part in the first assembly of the World Council of Indigenous Peoples, were dismayed to find that serious doubt was being cast on their credentials.

Not all Sami, in the past, lived off reindeer. Some, along the Norwegian coast, relied on fishing. Others worked small farms and picked berries, but the majority were herdsmen who relied on the animals for milk and annually killed a proportion of the herd for meat.

Like the Inuit, the Sami utilised all parts of the carcass: the skins for clothes and tents, the antlers for tools and domestic utensils.

Today, only ten per cent of the Sami earn their living from reindeer, annually slaughtering one-fifth of the herd for the domestic meat industry and supplementing their income from the sale of pelts and antlers to tourists.

Such are the economics of reindeer husbandry that in order to be wholly dependent on reindeer, a Sami family would need approximately 350 animals.

Most families now own fewer than 200 animals and rely on secondary occupations to improve their income. In Norway and Sweden, only 14 families have more than 300 animals; 25 families who listed reindeer herding as their principal occupation owned no reindeer at all.

Reindeer roundup, Troms, Norway.

Despite this decline, reindeer husbandry remains the keystone of Sami culture, closely linked with the Sami language.

Just as the Inuit language, Inuktitut, contains many words for the different characteristics of snow and ice, Sami has a rich vocabulary to describe a reindeer, words that take into account the physical condition, age, colour and shape of an animal, and the size of its antlers.

The language reflects the importance of reindeer to Sami society and acts as a cohesive element between families living in the traditional Sami lifestyle.

Reindeer herding also binds the families together and thus isolates them from outside influences. As well as being fundamental to the preservation of the language, these two elements are crucial to the survival of the Sami as a separate race. Both are severely threatened.

With no official status, the Sami language is rapidly succumbing to the dominant Nordic languages, which are used in administration, offices, schools and the media. Consequently, five per cent of reindeer herding Sami have no knowledge of their own language.

A study in Sweden shows that another 20 per cent cannot speak it, 45 per cent cannot read it, and 80 per cent cannot write it.

The figures for Sami who do *not* herd reindeer are even more alarming: 20 per cent have no knowledge of the language, 40 per cent cannot speak it, 65 per cent cannot read it, and 80 per cent cannot write it.

As the language falls into disuse, reindeer husbandry, the linchpin of Sami culture, is also under pressure from every quarter. Excessive forest felling, new roads and tourism have drastically reduced the grazing and, more importantly, the calving grounds.

Military authorities have requisitioned forest and tundra for training zones and artillery ranges. Engineers working on hydroelectric schemes have flooded valleys, re-routed rivers and disrupted reindeer migration routes.

Further anxiety stems from plans to extend the North Sea oil fields and lay pipelines through Samiland to take natural gas to West Germany.

The effect of these actions, instigated by business managers clearly indifferent to the complexities of reindeer husbandry, is devastating.

Indeed, the threat is so great that unless the encroachment into Samiland is contained very quickly, reindeer husbandry in the wild will become extinct, probably sooner rather than later. If that happens, the Sami culture is doomed.

Decision-makers in the south have failed to understand the difficulties of reindeer management and the hazards of the annual migratory cycle of reindeer. As mentioned earlier, to be economically viable, a herd must consist of approximately 350 animals and to keep track of them, the Sami now use snowmobiles and two-way radios.

As in Canada and Alaska, the snowmobiles are a mixed blessing. Costing more than one quarter of the value of a reindeer, they can seldom be driven for more than two winters, after which they are traded in for approximately six per cent of a reindeer's value.

During the time a machine is in a Sami's possession, it will probably consume 350 gallons of fuel a season, wear out four belts and require numerous expensive spare parts.

Sami herder, Finland.   Author's photograph

In one community, maintenance and fuel for snowmobiles was estimated at 90 per cent of the total income from reindeer husbandry.

The high cost of maintaining snowmobiles has forced some Sami to take second jobs in order to keep their machines and has led to an increase in the slaughter of animals, particularly of calves.

The effect of this has been to saturate the meat market, force prices down and reduce profit margins. Other difficulties arise from sudden, heavy rainfalls followed by a sharp drop in temperature which freezes the snow and prevents the animals reaching their winter fodder.

There have been lean winters during which the Sami have lost half their stock and emergency food for the remainder has been so expensive that by summer the animals have eaten their entire commercial value.

Reindeer husbandry is thus a hard way to earn a living. The Sami are not instinctively nomadic. Indeed, those who live by farming and fishing are sedentary. Reindeer herders, on the other hand, travel along specific routes to the summer and winter pastures, whenever possible using the same camps as for the previous year.

They follow the migratory cycle of their animals, a pattern which takes them on long journeys to the mountains in conditions which are often appalling, and always fraught with problems.

Reindeer feeding on lichen in winter. Author's photograph

In winter, the reindeer roam free through the partially forested tundra, where they dig through snow four feet deep in order to reach the moss and lichens which are their staple winter diet.

The snow protects the fodder from their hooves. If they lingered in the forests after the spring melt, they would crush the lichen, which dries out in summer and can take fifty years to flower, thus destroying their principal source of winter food for the following year. By April or May, the animals become restive and begin their instinctive migration to the calving grounds near the rivers, lakes and marshes.

Here, the snow melts more quickly, revealing the first green plants of the year. Rich in proteins, these young shoots are essential for the cows, which, undernourished after the long winter, have only a few weeks in which to gain weight and produce milk for their offspring. If they stay too long, the calves drown in rivers swollen by melting snow.

As if to spur the animals on, the mosquitoes hatch. By late May or early June, when the birch trees burst into leaf, the reindeer huddle together in an effort to escape the swarms.

It is now that the Sami separate them into herds, brand the fawns and drive the animals as far as 150 miles to their summer pastures in the mountains and along the northern coast of Norway, where the wind offers the animals some respite.

Here they remain until the autumn, when they are rounded up again and approximately one-fifth of the herd is selected for slaughter. In September and October when the rut occurs, the reindeer are driven back to their winter grazing and allowed to disperse as the first snow falls.

The highly-strung reindeer are liable to stampede at the sound of people, dogs and especially gunfire, vehicles and machinery. When the ground is free from snow, the herds can move faster than the herdsmen, who must be able to predict the movements of their animals, and find them in darkness, fog or blizzards.

Animals mingling with other herds travelling along parallel routes in the same direction can delay the migration, with dire results for calving and rutting. If the autumn round up is impeded or the peace vital for a successful rut is disturbed, late pregnancies can lead to miscarriages, delays to the spring migration and the death of calves.

Reindeer are so sensitive that they will shy away from areas where they have been frightened, avoiding them for as long as ten years and forcing the herders to find new migratory routes.

This can be a difficult, if not impossible, task when outside interests are continually encroaching on grazing lands. Forest felling can be particularly disruptive. The demand for timber is unceasing.

Huge tracts of forest are razed to the ground, destroying the moss and lichen. In north and eastern Finland, cleared forestland stretches as far as the eye can see, a barren landscape studded with dried tree stumps.

Autumn roundup, Troms, Norway. Author's photograph

Where replanting is carried out, the ground is first ploughed deeply, and trenched by heavy machinery. The forest floor becomes impassible, a tangle of roots and undergrowth.

The growth of lichen is halted and the reindeer are frightened away, perhaps forever. The destruction of winter grazing increases the pressure on other forestland, creating shortages of winter fodder, which may lead to the death of reindeer from starvation in the late winter and early spring.

Nor is this a short-term problem. A ploughed area may be useless for decades. Whereas pine trees in the south require between sixty and seventy years to mature, the same process north of the Arctic Circle can take between 150 and 250 years.

Yet, during a depression in the paper and pulp industry, Swedish businessmen deliberately increased the rate of forest clearance in order to prevent redundancies.

At the same time, they postponed replanting because demand was temporarily low, a policy of incredible shortsightedness. The effect of such decisions is inevitable. Each year, the total forest area in Samiland diminishes.

More forests have been obliterated by hydroelectric schemes, especially in Norway where fast flowing rivers provide more power than in any other country.

ultra

Further major projects are planned in all three Nordic countries. In Norwegian Samiland, the threat posed by one scheme was so great that it threatened to disrupt the calving grounds, migration routes and rutting areas of 40,000 animals.

Secondary chaotic effects, such as the *intermingling* of herds and increased pressure on other grazing lands, cannot be quantified. The scheme, known as the Alta-Kautokeino project, jeopardised the whole future of reindeer pastoralism in the heart of Samiland, with dire effects for the Sami language and culture.

The Alta River passes through the village of Kautokeino, the unofficial capital of Samiland, in which Sami is the mother tongue of more than eighty per cent of the 2,000 villagers.

Downstream, the river runs through Masi village, one of the most important centres for reindeer husbandry in the region and one of the last in the world where Sami is spoken by the entire population.

In 1970, Norway's State Water and Energy Development Authority (NVE) announced plans to dam the river and to create several reservoirs. The intention was to submerge a 25-mile stretch of river valley, including the village of Masi.

Alta River and Masi village. Author's photograph

Although protests by local people, who had not been consulted, eventually forced a substantial reduction in the scheme, the plans to regulate the water course placed the livelihoods of about 30 Masi households in jeopardy and threatened the loss of spring pasture.

The acreage involved was relatively small, but the grazing land was vital because there were no other suitable calving grounds in the vicinity.

Further difficulties arose from the topography of the region. With summer and winter grazing areas at opposite ends of the migration route, herds of between a few hundred and several thousand reindeer, totaling nearly 40,000 animals, had to travel through a gap far too narrow to allow them all through at the same time.

To avoid congestion, the Sami stagger the movement of the herds. This operation is especially complex after the autumn round-up. The Sami release the herds from their pens one by one, but by mid-September, with the rut approaching, it is difficult to restrain the animals.

To do so indefinitely would merely cause them to stampede through the barriers, fan out and mingle with other herds in the bottleneck.

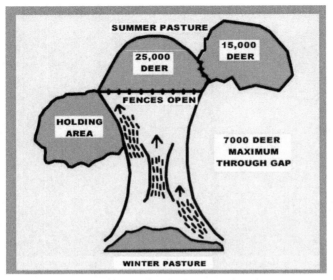

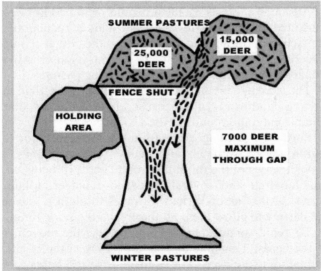

The Sami prevent this by driving some of the herds into special waiting zones, until there is room enough to move them through the gap.

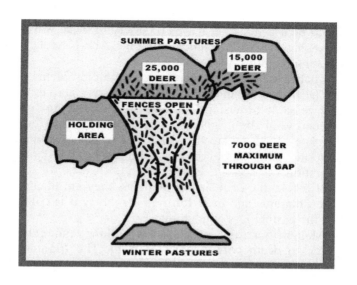

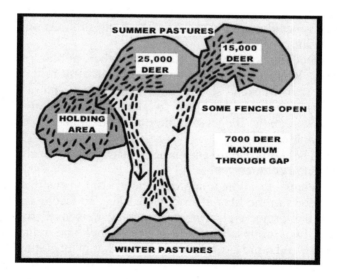

These zones are crucial because they allow the animals to graze without fear of disturbance for several weeks prior to, and during, the rut.

This is essential if late pregnancies and their effects

are to be avoided. Yet it was precisely in these waiting areas that the NVE planners sited the Alta-Kautokeino dam and 22 miles of access roadway.

Such disruption can create insuperable problems for the herdsmen. Reindeer alarmed by noise and traffic lose valuable browsing time and expend large amounts of energy on flight, giving rise to a protein deficiency which must be replaced quickly if the cows and their offspring are to be strong enough for the spring migration.

If the source of their fear remains, they are likely to desert the area and head for the hills where it is colder, and the pasture less nourishing.

Malnutrition and miscarriages follow, and calves freeze to death within hours of birth. The frightened animals will not return until long after the workers and their machines have disappeared.

It was twelve years before the Sami could persuade a herd to cross the approach road to one newly constructed dam and use prime calving grounds on the far side.

Opening approach roads to the public after completion of a hydroelectric project usually brings an influx of weekend skiers, hunters, fishermen and tundra tourists whose arrival is frequently followed by an increase in the illegal slaughter of reindeer and the theft of their carcasses.

The Alto- Kautokeino scheme posed a further threat to Sami culture.

Plans to billet approximately 200 construction workers in the Masi district were likely to lead, as with similar projects elsewhere, to sexual liaisons between the two groups, illicit deals in alcohol and reindeer meat, and rapid assimilation into the dominant culture.

Previous experience indicated that some herdsmen might be given temporary jobs on the project, but that instead of using their earnings to buy reindeer, they would develop new habits and needs, and fritter the money away.

*The reindeer roundup and
Sami herdsmen.*

When the dam was completed, the Sami would be out of work and, disillusioned and discontented, be obliged to live on social welfare. With enforced retirement a certainty for most of the reindeer herders in the Alta River region, the Sami began to organise themselves into protest groups. Their demonstrations led to a marked reduction in the size of the scheme and the threat of flooding Masi village was removed.

Nevertheless, the NVE still intended to blast tunnels through the mountainside, and build a 350-ft high dam of reinforced concrete, a power station and an approach road.

But the Norwegian parliament declared Masi an area of national heritage, in consequence of which, the NVE commissioned an investigation into the harm that might result from the project and the appropriate rates of compensation for those affected.

For the NVE itself to do this was as cynical as a tobacco company setting up a study into the effects of cigarettes on health and then determining the amount of compensation payable to the victims of cigarette-induced cancer.

The terms of reference required the investigating team to consider only the direct damages likely to result from the Alta-Kautokeino scheme.

Its brief was to map and register migration routes and pastureland, and assess the compensation for their loss. No directive was given and no attempt was made to find out why the area was of such importance, or to instruct parliament about the wider implications of the project for reindeer management.

It has been compared with removing a stave from a wine barrel and assessing the damage as a percentage of lost wood. Furthermore, the commission based its report on the original, more ambitious Alta- Kautokeino project.

When the smaller plan was adopted, the authorities falsely assumed that the damage to reindeer pastoralism would be reduced proportionately and thus be negligible.

The commission did note that the loss of valuable calving grounds would be 'very serious' and reported that every additional loss of pasture was likely to have catastrophic consequences, even when a loss was only for a limited period.

The Norwegian parliament chose to ignore this in a debate that minimized the problem:

"So far as reindeer pastoralism is concerned," observed one speaker, "the only loss would be the flooding of some pastures. Their value approximates to food for 21 reindeer for 115 days."

The compensation was calculated accordingly.

Incensed, the Sami organised a protest camp near Alta, attracting several thousand Sami, farmers and environmentalists not only from all over Scandinavia but also the rest of Europe.

Masi Dam.

Author's photograph.

Linking themselves together with chains, they halted all work on the approach road for nearly four months.

In the meantime, another group of Sami travelled to Oslo, set up camp outside the parliament building and began a hunger strike.

Politically embarrassed, the Prime Minister announced that the whole project would be re-examined, but the government's attitude became apparent shortly afterwards when an ill-informed deputy minister, quoting woefully incorrect statistics, declared:

> 'There is no connection between Sami interests and the Alta-Kautokeino hydro project. The whole project affects, as far as I can remember, no more than the equivalent of the pasture as needed by eight or ten animals over one year, and that is not much in view of the 140,000 reindeer in Finnmark [Norwegian Samiland].'

The hearing by the Norwegian Court of Appraisal was most noteworthy for the discrepancies between the evidence it accepted and the conclusions drawn from it. The court agreed that the spring pastures could not be replaced, that the calving grounds and waiting zones would be lost, and that this amounted to a serious incursion into the pattern of reindeer management in the area. With that firmly established, the court concluded:

'It seems doubtful that the incursions we have mentioned are of such proportion and of such significance as to be of any important consequence to Sami culture... The investigation that has been undertaken is satisfactory in respect of those damages that have been considered'.

As if to add insult to injury, the Court added that Masi was not an area of national heritage after all, and that the proposal to make it one had been made on the floor of parliament, not in parliamentary committee, and was therefore not legally binding.

At a subsequent hearing, the Supreme Court upheld the state on all essential points. It rejected arguments that the evidence placed before lower courts was inadequate and misleading, and ruled that the potential effect of the Alta-Kautokeino project on reindeer management was not sufficiently serious to bring parliament's decision into conflict with international common law.

Compensation, it decided, should be paid only on the basis of lost acreage.

Moreover, the Sami affected by the project could not be considered an indigenous people because the river was being regulated in a region that came under Norwegian jurisdiction.

This was all the government needed. With the support of parliament, approval was given to commence work on the project, which had been halted for more than a year.

Bitterly disappointed, about 1,000 Sami and their sympathisers returned to the protest camp. As they chained themselves to boulders strewn along the access road, the temperature dropped to, 35°C (-31°F).

The Sami, wearing their traditional pompom hats and colourful costumes, threatened to freeze themselves to death. The government response was to embark on the biggest and most expensive peacetime police action ever.

At a cost of £100,000 (approx. $150.000) a day, 600 police officers were flown to the site with their dogs in a fleet of chartered aircraft.

A large passenger ferry anchored off the Norwegian coast, 25 miles away, to house them. In shifts of 200 men, the police worked day and night, cutting chains and transporting the demonstrators through the snow to the court at Alta, where they were fined about £300 ($450) each. Most of the Sami refused to pay and returned to the camp as quickly as possible, but soon the last protestors were removed.

Later, fourteen Sami women were granted permission to discuss the issue with the Prime Minister, but dissatisfied with the government's argument that more electric power was needed to create new industry, and that the Sami would have to pay the price, they refused to leave and police were called in to remove them.

At the same time, five Sami herdsmen embarked on a hunger strike that lasted 31 days.

Another Sami, who had become an activist, attempted to sabotage the hydroelectric project by blowing up a bridge. Unfortunately, the charges detonated prematurely and he lost an eye and a hand. It was the last protest.

A month before the injured Sami was due for trial, he fled to Canada. The Alta-Kautokeino dam had become a symbol of Sami defeat.

In Swedish Samiland, the Sami suffered another setback when the Supreme Court refused to recognise the right of eleven Sami villages to ownership of approximately 4,000 square miles close to the Norwegian border. The decision concluded a court case that had lasted nineteen years, the longest in Swedish legal history.

Claiming that roads, railways and increased tourism were threatening their lifestyle and culture, the Sami were seeking greater control over development of the region. Among the documentation considered by the court was a royal decree from the 17th century.

This not only gave the Sami title to the territory, but also promised them the right to control it for all eternity.

Despite this, the court held that as a semi-nomadic people they could not acquire the right of ownership over a territory which, throughout history, they had formally failed to claim.

Official thinking on Samiland was placed into perspective when the Governor of Finnmark (Norwegian Samiland) commented: 'In this day and age, the tundra areas of our province are, *first and foremost,* important as recreational areas... particularly for the week-end tourist.'

Sami at Kautokeino wedding on Norwegian-Swedish border. Author's photograph

His comment underlined the rule which has enabled the industrial monoculture to steamroll its way over lesser cultures in every part of the world, that when the advantages to the larger, urban population are greater than the disadvantages to smaller, rural groups, all schemes are socially defensible, irrespective of the damage to the individual or the countryside.

When construction on the Alta-Kautokeino dam commenced, the Sami attempted to drive their reindeer along a more northerly route to the summer pastures. As expected, the herds intermingled.

During a subsequent election campaign, the

Norwegian Minister for the Environment expressed the personal view that, had the effects of the dam on reindeer management and the Sami culture been fully appreciated, permission to build the dam would have been withheld.

As if the Sami did not have enough problems, in

1986, a nuclear reactor called Chernobyl blew up. Within a few hours of the explosion, south easterly winds carried clouds of radioactive dust from Russia to the heart of Samiland and contaminated the tundra.

Lichen in northern Norway

You could not see. this contamination. Nor could you smell it. Nor even feel, touch, taste or hear it. But it was there, permeating the mosses and lichens.

With no root system, lichens take their nutrition from the atmosphere and so they soaked up the radioactive Caesium like a sponge. With a half-life of 28 years, it did not disappear completely until the year 2014.

Immediately after Chernobyl, the reindeer were found to be carrying deadly amounts of Caesium in their bodies, between ten and 80,000 bequerels per kilo, compared with a permissible limit of just 600. In Sweden and Norway, the Sami had to slaughter and bury some 60,000 contaminated reindeer.

The following year, in 1987, that number dropped sharply, primarily because the Norwegian authorities raised the safety limit from 600 to 6000 bequerels per kilo.

Even so, in some areas as many as one in five reindeer were deemed unfit for human consumption, and had to be put down.

Raising the safety limit meant that about 75% of the reindeer meat, which previously would have been unfit for human consumption, could now be sold and eaten.

The Norwegian authorities said radiation levels in animals and humans would increase "only marginally". However, they did not take into account that many Sami ate reindeer meat every day, and sometimes several times a day, or that they had no Geiger counters and could not therefore tell if they were eating more than the recommended limits.

So, it was impossible to calculate the long-term effects. Happily, at least so far as we know, there appear not to have been too many so far.

Nevertheless, more than 100,000 more reindeer had to be put down during the next five years. Today, all reindeer meat intended for the domestic and foreign markets is subjected to stringent laboratory tests.

Measuring Caesium levels in reindeer, Troms,
Norway. Author's photograph

Any meat showing more than 6,000 bequerels per kilo is rejected.

For the Sami people, of course, Chernobyl was just one more devastating blow. The grave concern at the time was that the effects of radioactivity ingested in small doses over a long period of time might take years to appear. Nobody knew what would happen. Indeed, we still don't know with absolute certainty that there will be no adverse effects on the Sami people, although now it does look hopeful.

Today, the threat to the Sami people and their culture is still very considerable and unless encroachment is contained very quickly, reindeer husbandry in the wild, even for the 'wealthier' herders, will become extinct. If that happens, the Sami culture is doomed.

Tourism is vital to many Sami. Author's photograph

Is there a way out of this predicament? Clearly, it is not possible to turn back so-called progress, but it *is* possible to approach the future with greater caution. Tourism may provide a solution.

Visitors to Samiland invariably visit other parts of Norway, too, and thus feed money into the Norwegian economy. More importantly, tourism is a secondary source of income crucial to the survival of many Sami people.

Slowly, life *is* changing for the better. Whereas the Sami were once denied their language, church services now have double pulpits and simultaneous translation, all subsidised by the state. Today, the Sami have their own parliament., although it has no powers.

It can't pass any laws and the state remains adamant that the Sami will always be Norwegians first and Sami second. But they have gradually given them greater autonomy, at least concerning those aspects of life that are most important to them.

The Alta dam politicised the Sami and taught them to stand up for themselves. It taught the Norwegians that the Sami culture is their heritage, too.

Today, Sami children can study in their own language, at their own schools, until they reach their teens and although there is still a serious shortage of Sami textbooks, they can then go on to Sami University.

Today, the Sami people have their own radio-and-television station, and their own newspaper, each playing a vital role in preserving the Sami language and thus the Sami culture.

Today, Sami who live in the Nordic capitals, working in every sector of society, are making renewed efforts to revive, to strengthen and to pass on to future generations their cultural heritage.

Today, the protection of Sami rights and the Sami language are guaranteed and today, the Sami of Samiland have their own flag and their own anthem, but still not their own land.

Yet, thanks to the Alta dam, today they are able once again to wear their traditional costumes with a renewed sense of pride.

So, the question is: Can the Sami culture can survive?

The answer must be a resounding 'yes' provided that the decision-makers in the south show restraint and common sense, and develop a greater sensitivity to the needs of the Sami people.

Lutheran priest and Sami woman, Kautokeino

Much will depend on the younger generation of Sami people, too. It used to be said that if you were lost in the forest, all you had to do was to look for the moss on a tree and you would know in which direction north lay.

Today, even in Samiland, you need look only at the corners of the houses and see the satellite dishes, which always point sou'-southwest!

Television and the influence it brings from afar has helped to create a discontent amongst young Sami, as it has among the Inuit and other indigenous peoples, so that they are tempted to leave home for the cities and a more modern lifestyle

The Sami Future: Will they just be part of a cultural zoo?

In the case of the Sami people, however, it is gratifying to realise that, time after time, young people are discovering that city life is not quite what they thought. And in them lies hope because now, for the first time, they are beginning to return, in considerable numbers, to the last great wilderness of Europe.

***

Svalbard: A Final Frontier

Julian Huxley, the English evolutionary biologist, author, humanist and internationalist, described the approach to Spitzbergen, from the sea in this way:

'The view was indeed beautiful," he wrote, "with glittering patches of drift-ice and straight ahead, the mountains after which Spitsbergen is named, sharp-pointed peaks with snow on their upper flanks, rather as if the top four thousand feet of the Alps had been cut off and transplanted to the Arctic Ocean'.

This photograph illustrates what he meant:

Svalbard was discovered – or rather re-discovered, by the Dutch explorer, William Barents, who landed on Spitzbergen in 1596.

'Re-discovered' because a record in the Icelandic Sagas from 1194, 400 years earlier, refers to a country named Svalbard with "cold coasts which had been discovered by Vikings".

By that time, of course, the Vikings had already colonised Iceland and Greenland, and discovered North America. Indeed, the Vikings actually believed that Svalbard was a continuation of Greenland.

The first people known to have spent a winter on the Svalbard islands were eight crazy Britons in 1630.

They declared the islands uninhabitable because they lay within what in those days was known as the "Zona Frigida". Contemporary 17th century records state that the climate "is so rough that the animals are completely white". One blanches at the mere thought of it!

Conditions in winter can certainly be severe. After all, the islands lie only 700 miles (1,300 kilometres) from the North Pole and roughly the same distance north of the Arctic Circle.

Svalbard is a land of extremes. In March 1986, meteorologists reported a record low temperature at Longyearbyen Airport of minus 46° Celsius. That's minus 51° Fahrenheit.

In July, it is just six degrees Centigrade or 43° Fahrenheit. and the temperature will rarely exceed 12°C (53°F).

From April to August, the sun never sets, but from mid-November to February, it remains below the horizon, casting the islands into constant darkness.

Svalbard is a Norwegian dependency and consists of cluster of glaciated islands, bounded by the Arctic Ocean, the Barents Sea, the Greenland Sea and the Norwegian Sea.

The largest island is Spitzbergen, which has more than 60 per cent of the total land area of about 24,000 square miles. With a resident population of about 3,000 people, that means on average that there are some 8,000 square miles to each individual – roughly the size of Lichtenstein.

However, with the exception of about a dozen licensed hunters who live an extraordinary lonely existence, Svalbard residents tended to live in four main settlements: Longyearbyen, Barentsburg, Pyramiden, and Sveagruva. All mining towns.

They did so out of necessity rather than choice because the islands mostly comprise wild and rugged mountains, with much of the high land covered in ice.

Like Norway, the coast is indented with several large fjords, particularly along the west and north coasts.

So, outside the settlements, it's about as wild and as desolate a place as you could possibly hope to find.

Indeed, in describing the way the land is used, the CIA World Fact Book notes that:

- arable land amounts to zero per cent
- permanent crops – zero per cent
- meadows and pastures – zero per cent
- forest and woodland – zero per cent. There are no trees and the only bushes are crowberry and cloudberry

The other 100 per cent comprises mountains, glaciers, tundra and boggy marshland, and not much else.

The darkest phase of Svalbard's peacetime history came with the arrival of the whalers in the mid-18th century. Whaling had been an important source of income since the mid-18th century and in the capitals of Europe, the whalers and their cargoes were awaited eagerly.

Once whales had been sighted, vessels from Holland, Britain, Germany and Scandinavia all headed north to Svalbard intent on butchery. Their prey was the bowhead, or Greenland whale – 70 feet long and weighing 60 tons.

This cumbersome creature could yield 20 tons of oil and was thus a prime source of food, fuel and light.

At the height of the season, some 450 ships and approximately 20,000 men were employed by the Svalbard industry.

The continual daylight of the arctic summer allowed men to work shifts day and night; The outcome was inevitable.

Eventually, the stocks of bowhead whales dwindled and were depleted to what, euphemistically, was described as "commercial extinction".

But even after that, the hunting continued until all the whale populations in Svalbard waters, every single whale – had been exterminated. Consequently, some of the whalers, notably the Norwegians, Instead turned to hunting seals and walrus.

The "sea cows", as walrus were known then, could weigh more than a ton and were valued for their ivory tusks, thick hides and oil.

The skin of a bull could be an inch thick and was especially prized as the best material for shields and armour, and later for bicycle seats.

The oil was used to seal ship's planking, the ivory was considered perfect for toilet accessories for women and in satisfying these markets, walruses were massacred with abandon throughout the Arctic.

In less than a decade, so many walruses had been killed that there were no longer enough left to warrant the expense of another voyage.

Later, in 1899, coal was discovered. This proved to be the turning point in the development of the islands, unleashing in northern Europe a situation not unlike the Klondike.

Many ill-conceived mining ventures failed to make a profit – but in 1905, John M. Longyear, a colourful mine-owner from Michigan in the United States, founded the Arctic Coal Company, which was subsequently taken over by the Norwegian State.

JOHN MUNRO LONGYEAR 1850 - 1922
LONGYEARBYENS GRUNNLEGGER 1906

Longyear, of course, also gave his name to the main settlement on Svalbard, Longyearbyen – the Norwegian suffix *'byen'* meaning 'the town'.

Today, coal is no longer being mined in Longyearbyen. The Norwegians brought it to a halt in 2017 after 100 years of operation on the grounds that it was no longer economical.

Although American, British, Dutch and Swedish coal companies had mined in the past, the only companies mining coal today are Russian.

Their output is minimal. The Russian mine at Pyramiden and the Swedish Sveagruven mine are also closed, not least because after 2008, coal prices plummeted from $160 dollars a ton to less than $45 dollars a ton.

Although there are deposits of copper, iron ore, phosphate and zinc on the Svalbard islands, coal was always the sole exploited mineral.

What little coal is produced at the Russian mine at Barentsburg is primarily a statement, an excuse for a political presence on the islands, because whoever holds Spitzbergen controls entry and exit to the Barents Sea – Russia's only gateway to the Atlantic.

Aside from the economics and environmental concerns about mining, closure of the mines is probably a good thing because it was a rotten job: the temperature in the mines, particularly in wintertime, could be as low as minus 15° or 20° Centigrade.

Under a League of Nations Treaty signed in 1920, it was agreed that Norway should have absolute and unlimited sovereignty over Svalbard.

The islands were demilitarised and all of the 40 signatory nations received equal rights to exploit mineral deposits subject to Norwegian regulations.

Norway, however, unilaterally claims a 120-mile (200 kilometre) exclusive fishing zone around the archipelago.

This is hotly contested by Russia and it remains an international dispute that has been running for years.

Russia's concern is based on the possibility that they might be excluded from sinking exploratory oil and gas wells in those areas where geologists believe they are most likely to be successful.

There have been several successful gas strikes, which is often seen as an indicator that oil, too, is present. Needless to say, this is a matter of great concern to environmentalists who are aware of the extremely sensitive nature of the Arctic environment.

If oil were to be discovered, it would not be difficult to imagine the scramble and the international wrangling that would result with 40 signatory nations each with equal mineral rights.

Nor would it be especially challenging to envisage the effect the oil industry would have on an environment that is arguably the most sensitive and vulnerable in the world.

Many cruise ships call in at Ny Ålesund, (pronounced *nee-awly-soond* as opposed to *Nye Ah-lesund* or *Ali-sund*) a small settlement that lies in Kongsfjord (which means 'King's Fjord).

A few years ago, it was little more than a handful of wooden buildings housing an equally small number of research workers and scientists.

Today, with the growth of scientific research on the island, it has become a small town complete with a new hotel in case you miss your ship.

There is also a tourist shop as well stocked as any in Norway and a post office which offers a certain kudos to be gained from posting your cards, given that this is the world's most northerly post office.

Concerns about the risk to the environment posed by ships burning heavy fuel, however, has resulted in the Norwegians banning such ships from sailing into the fjord.

A memorial to Roald Amundsen commemorates his visit in 1926, when he arrived in an airship which he tethered to a pylon before flying to Alaska via the North Pole 700 miles away, the first trans-polar flight ever.

Ny Ålesund is also one of the main nesting sites for thousands of Arctic terns. These remarkable birds fly from the Antarctic to Svalbard and back again. Every Year, a round trip of 24,000 miles!

The terns must recover from those journeys, nest, breed and raise their young in just 12 short weeks of Arctic summer.

So, it is of paramount importance that we humans should not disturb them. The problem is that they nest everywhere, often just at the side of the road and walkways. Not surprisingly, the birds will defend their young with great vigour and determination, and visitors are sometimes surprised when they walk past a nest and discover to their horror that they are under ferocious attack, with male birds often drawing blood with their sharp bills.

Some cruise ships give passengers a stick about three feet long to hold above their heads so that the birds attack the stick rather than the passengers' heads.

Sadly, some passengers use the sticks in an effort to beat the birds off. It is an equally sad fact that ships' cruise staff all too often have no knowledge of these facts with which to keep passengers properly informed.

As mentioned previously, the darkest period of Svalbard's peacetime history was the whaling era.

Far worse, of course, were the events on Svalbard during the Second World War, when British, German and Norwegian forces all occupied the islands.

In August 1941, allied troops were sent north to Spitzbergen, where – at the time – some 4,000 miners were continuing to dig out the coal in spite of the war in Europe.

The allies were keen to prevent the coal mines falling into German hands, so they decided to evacuate the miners and disable the mines.

Barely three weeks after the last allied ship had left, German troops landed on Spitzbergen and they came not to take over the mines, but to set up meteorological stations to gather vital weather information for the German Airforce and Navy.

These weather stations were ranked in importance even higher than Germany's submarine forces, so they were clearly considered vital and this information – flying conditions, visibility at sea and so on – soon paid off, not least for German Air Force pilots attacking the Allied convoys to Russia.

Time and again, the ships were attacked by German pilots supplied with information from the arctic weather men on Spitzbergen

When Allied spies stole secret documents that revealed German plans to expand their bases on Spitzbergen, Churchill gave the go-ahead to reoccupy the island.

In May 1942, a force of 83 Norwegian troops and three British observers arrived off the coast of Spitzbergen in two small ships. They found their way blocked by solid ice and were soon spotted by a German supply plane that called in four Fokke Wolfs.

Fourteen men were killed in the attack. The remaining troops struggled across the ice to Barentsburg. Most of their supplies had gone down with the ships, so for six weeks they had to survive on whatever they could scavenge in the deserted town.

Finally, two British battleships arrived bringing troops from the Scottish Brigade, many of them former miners from Spitzbergen.

It was a strange, secret war fought by a small number of men on a huge island.

For almost two years, the Germans maintained a weather station high up in the mountains in the northwest of the island.

When, eventually, they were discovered, Hitler decided to get rid of the Norwegians once and for all – and he ordered the battleships *Tirpitz* and *Scharnhorst* to Spitzbergen with a fleet of ten destroyers.

In just six hours, German navy artillery and troops had left Longyearbyen in ruins.

Six Norwegians were killed and 41 were taken prisoner, but within a year, the allies had sunk most of the German ships that had taken part in the assault. Such is war!

The Germans, meanwhile, managed to relay their weather information right through to the end of the war.

Afterwards, the relentless militarisation of the Arctic continued with the advent of intercontinental ballistic missiles, the DEW line and the Cold War. Today, Svalbard, and Longyearbyen particularly, is very different.

About 3,000 inhabitants are currently living on the Svalbard archipelago and all of them, including the Russians, come under the jurisdiction of the Norwegian governor, who is known as the _Sysselman._

His or her responsibilities include overseeing Norway's rights and duties as described in the Svalbard Treaty.

The _Sysselman's_ office is also responsible for:

...fish and wildlife services

...pollution and oil spill protection...

... environmental monitoring...

... warden services

... commercial development

... and, of course, since the _Sysselman_ is essentially a police officer, for fighting crime.

It's a highly varied job and certainly one aspect of it became apparent in August 1996, when a Russian airliner crashed six miles east of Longyearbyen in the worst airline disaster ever on Norwegian soil.

The tragedy struck the Russian mining communities at Barentsburg and Pyramiden particularly hard. There were no survivors among the 141 people aboard, all of whom apart from the 12 crew and four children, were miners.

The aircraft was a long way off course from the normal approach to the airfield and heavy fog, winds and snow on the plateau made rescue work for the _Sysselman,_ 40 Norwegians and 15 Russians extremely difficult.

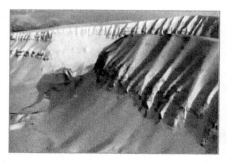

There was some criticism that it took nearly a week to retrieve and identify the bodies. When you see the terrain, it is not hard to see why.

In this part of the world, it is nature, not the human being, that prevails. For the 600 Russians in Barentsburg, life is bleak, reminders of the Cold War never far away. A bust of Lenin still reigns supreme.

Once, exhortations to work adorned the Barentsburg theatre. Now, the state murals have gone.

Plays about work ethics are no more and most of the buildings have been repainted or clad with fascinating mosaics. Occasionally, the miners and their families produce incredibly moving productions for the few cruise ships that come here.

Sports are the main activities. The water in the Olympic sized pool is a touch green – unlike some of the dying plants.

Basketball is very popular. Off-duty miners practise every day, preparing for a busy fixtures list. Soccer likewise. Indeed, sports activities are just about the only form of entertainment in Barentsburg.

It's a frontier town that for years looked and felt run down, permeated with poverty and grim despondency. There was no double glazing, only plastic sheeting to keep out the cold.

Since then, there have been many improvements, although Barentsburg remains a desolate outpost.

At the dawn of the 21st century, conditions were dismal, to put it mildly. The miners at that time were rarely paid and often on long contracts from which there was no escape.

Local buses and trucks were, and still are, antiquated, barely able to struggle up the hill from the harbour and the state of the Aeroflot truck hardly inspires confidence in the airline.

Cruise ship passengers and souvenir sales became a crucial part of the economy for the near destitute miners and their families: in the local store, cold war relics were a speciality, samovars and Babushka dolls plentiful.

Today, the shop is as well stocked as any in Norway or elsewhere.

Food in the miners' canteen then was adequate, but plain and stodgy. That's because everything had to be imported mostly by sea when the harbour is ice-free.

Yet the Russians are an innovative people. They imported a handful of cattle and built a dairy to ensure fresh milk supplies. There weren't many cows, mainly because they had to kill off some cattle to provide meat when the supply ship didn't come.

When supplies failed to arrive the following year, the miners were forced to slaughter the remaining animals, including a calf in which they had immense pride.

It was the same with the greenhouse. The sparsity of supplies, particularly during winter, meant that green vegetables and salads were hard to come by.

Huge, strange looking bulbs helped them achieve impressive crops, particularly of tomatoes.

Nor were conditions in Pyramiden much different. With its dramatic mountain backdrop and view of the Nordenskiöld glacier, Pyramiden had a natural "wow" factor.

Today, it's a ghost town today, abandoned in a matter of months in 1998.

Equipment used for coal mining is exactly how the workers left it, mostly ready to go back into action at the push of a button. Photographs and documents litter the tables and cupboards in various rooms.

Residents lived in apartment blocks nicknamed 'London' for single men, and 'Paris' for the few women who lived here. Now, seagulls occupy the window sills to rear their young.

The projection room in the cinema is a mess of old 35mm film. A statue of Lenin dominates the main square. The Palace of Culture featured a swimming pool, now empty and abandoned, but once was considered the best in Svalbard. Even children from Longyearbyen came here.

There was a basketball court, a weight-lifting room, a library and a theatre in which residents could watch regular performances and movies.

Music was important, too. This is the piano, which the miners referred to as 'Red Oktober' and which was brought in by ship along with balalaikas, keyboards and accordions.

In short, it was meant to be a showcase for Soviet society. Pyramiden was a town where any foreigner could visit without a visa, so it served as an exhibition of the best the USSR had to offer, but the collapse of the Soviet Union in 1991 and the plane crash in 1996 took their toll. The population was devastated and depression set in.

Meanwhile, the Russian economy gradually became more unstable and because massive investment was needed to reach new and deeper levels of coal, the decision was made to close the mine. The last coal was extracted in March, 1998. By October, the entire population had abandoned it.

Sadly, since then many of the decorations and relics have been destroyed, strewn on the ground or stolen by tourists, and many of the public buildings have been vandalized.

That said, the Arctic environment acts very, very slowly and it has been estimated that the buildings here will still be standing in 500 years' time!

From time to time, arctic foxes *and* polar bears pass through. That makes it imperative to have a rifle-carrying guide: Be warned. Wandering off into the wild may seem safe, but is in fact extremely dangerous.

Longyearbyen, although just a few miles away across the fjord, is entirely different. There are several planes a day to and from the Norwegian mainland and it *feels* like any other town in Norway.

Communications are excellent. Longyearbyen is now an important centre for space research, tracking the ever-growing number of satellites in space and collecting and collating data from them.

The university and various research institutes have transformed Longyearbyen into a major centre for research, studying everything from animal and Arctic plant life to the ionosphere.

These studies, not coal, are now providing the *raison d'etre* for Norway's continued tenure in Svalbard.

Education is the same as in mainland Norway, with one difference. Longyearbyen boasts the only nursery school in the world with a protective polar bear fence.

Houses colours vary because when it's dark and snowing in winter it helps identify where you live. With only 12 miles of paved road in all Svalbard, snowmobiles and dog teams are the only form of transport other than by boat outside the town.

Dwarfed by old mine buildings, the Lutheran church is also a community centre where you can read *Svalbard Posten,* the town's local newspaper – or have a cup of coffee and write your postcards. It even has its own polar bear. More on *that* later on.

The lectern cloth seemed to sum up what the church was all about but sadly they decided to take it down and it now resides in a cupboard, but the people there will show it to you if you ask.

Longyearbyen has changed dramatically in the past few years.

Once just a collection of wooden huts, it's now a tourist attraction and tourists don't always understand that polar bears *are* here and dangerous, a reminder that despite the banks, the post office, space research, supermarkets and the most northerly newspaper in the world, it is still a frontier town.

To be sure, the local shops are well stocked, not least with the ubiquitous polar bears that we, the tourists, rarely see. But they are there, all right. Even if most of them are just cuddly toys.

Cruise lines are guilty of deliberately featuring polar bears in their glossy public relations brochures, knowing full well that the chances of actually seeing a polar bear are very unlikely.

Having cruised to this part of the world for 25 years, I have only seen a polar bear one two occasions, both on the same day, further north in Magdalena Bay.

If you *do* see one, it will almost certainly be stranded, hungry and extremely perilous.

So, pay attention to the notices and under no circumstances stray from the town. Indeed, it is illegal to do so without a rifle or a companion with a rifle.

Remember, too, that you cannot outrun a polar bear. If annoyed or hungry, one can kill you with a single blow of its paw. Be warned.

You can, however, see stuffed polar bears in the church, in one of the shops and in the very interesting little museum, which depicts the arctic way of life for the miners, hunters, whalers, trappers and so on. It's well worth a visit.

Occasionally, cruise passengers have sparked all kinds of rumours, not to mention extremely ill-informed action campaigns about these stuffed polar bears.

Be assured that Norwegians are not getting the Canadians to kill polar bears for them. Nor is the Norwegian government about to permit killing polar bears.

In fact, nobody in the entire arctic region from Alaska to Northern Canada, Greenland, Svalbard or Russia can kill a polar bear without specific permission.

Even then, you may harm a bear only in line with *extremely* strict regulations and quota systems approved by the United Nations.

The *only* other time a polar bear may be killed is during a life-threatening emergency. In that event, the Norwegian *Sysselman* will require a major investigation, a lot of form filling and the possibility of extremely hefty fines if the emergency was deemed to have been caused by panic, rather than handled with reason.

***

The Resistance: Norway's
Paper Clip War

Norwegians are a peace-loving people, often at the forefront of United Nations peacekeeping operations around the world. There is good reason for this; they became fed up with war. They had, after all, been involved in countless wars on and off for well over a thousand years.

These ranged from local Viking wars to civil wars, a Seven-Year war, a 30-year-war, the Great Northern War, the Napoleonic wars and so on and so forth.

Not surprisingly, these various wars had made a serious indent into the nation's coffers. By 1918, they were thoroughly disgruntled with the whole business of conflict. It was one of the principal reasons why the Norwegian government decided to declare the country neutral during both World Wars.

Sadly, their desire for neutrality in 1940 was shattered; Germany considered both Sweden and Norway far too important to allow it.

The object of Hitler's interest was a massive complex of mines in northern Sweden that had been exporting high grade iron ore to Germany's steel mills and armaments factories These mines are among the largest iron ore mines in the world. At the beginning of the war, they were exporting 600,000 tons of high-grade ore to Germany.

The ore was processed to pellets and fines, which were then transported through the truly beautiful countryside of Swedish and Norwegian Lapland.

Today, tourists follow the same route on luxury trains with panoramic views.

Completed in 1902, the line passes through 21 tunnels and descends 520 metres over a distance of 24 miles (39 kilometres) to the harbour at Narvik on the north Norwegian coast.

Incidentally, the ore is becoming harder to extract and, in some cases, the miners have bored 1.24 miles (two kilometres) below the surface.

This has caused an immense crack to appear and it is heading directly towards the centre of Kiruna, the town which owes its existence to the mine in the first place.

Kiruna is a town of some 20,000 people, and it will have to be moved. This will be a mammoth project. To do it, engineers will have to move houses, shops, the church and the Town Hall.

It was in Narvik and the fjord beyond it that German ships waited to load the ore that was so vital for the German war machine and ship it south along Norway's 1,000-mile coast to German ports.

At the time, Hitler was deeply concerned, even convinced, that Britain and France might invade Norway and sever his supplies of iron ore, with the inevitable result that he would not be able to achieve his military goals.

Realising this, the commander of the German Navy, Grand Admiral Raeder, proposed that capturing coastal bases in Norway would create major problems for the British navy.

Hitler immediately concurred and, on the 9th April, 1940, Germany invaded. German troops immediately captured several coastal towns and by that evening, German soldiers were marching through the streets of Oslo, the Norwegian capital.

King Haakon refused to surrender and immediately left Oslo for the countryside with Crown Prince Olav and his wife Crown Princess Martha, travelling hither and thither as the Germans pursued them.

For several days, the 68-year-old king did not sleep and the trio remained on the run for some two months before they ended up in Molde on the west coast.

But Molde was also attacked and with the town in flames, the King and government officials boarded H.M.S. Glasgow and made their escape to London, where they set up a government in exile.

By now, the Germans controlled the entire length of the Norwegian coast and were thus able to protect the iron ore shipments, attack British sea lanes and later, the Arctic Convoys, at will.

Importantly, they were also now able to receive an uninterrupted supply of Swedish iron ore, with exports to Germany rising from 600,000 tons in 1940 to 1.8 million tons by 1943.

The German invasion stunned the peace-loving Norwegian people. They were understandably shocked to the core, confused, dejected and depressed.

Despite, or rather because, of what they considered the rape of their country, the vast majority of

Norwegians developed an intense hatred of the Nazi troops and all things German. Gradually, they turned to non-violent resistance.

It began in a very small way, by ridiculing the Germans, cracking insulting jokes and making up anecdotes about them and also by wearing paper clips on their lapels.

The paper clip was a Norwegian invention and although innocuous, when everybody began wearing one, it became a secret and powerful symbol that united the population against the occupation.

They also wore small coins with King Haakon's head brightly polished. They also marked his birthday by wearing 'loyalty flowers' and lapel pins comprising the symbol H7 (for King Haakon the Seventh).

It was an act of defiance and the Germans were not slow to exact punishment. Hundreds of people were arrested and imprisoned for this relative innocent offence.

As time went by, Norwegian attitudes hardened. Their initial shock and confusion morphed into what they described as presenting an 'ice front' to any German they saw or met.

They refused to speak to a German except when it could not be evaded. They pretended not to understand German, although the Germans knew full well that German was taught in Norwegian schools and was certainly as prevalent in the country then as English is today.

No Norwegian (other than Quislings) would sit next to a German on buses and trams. The German authorities were incensed by this and eventually made it illegal to stand on a bus if seats were available.

The day after the German invasion, on 10th April, Vidkun Quisling, the leader of Norway's Nazi party, declared himself to be Prime Minister. Most Norwegians thought it was laughable – but not funny.

Quisling served as a nominal head of the Norwegian government from 1942 to 1945, although in fact he was very much under the thumb of a new "Reichskommissar", Josef Terboven.

He immediately brought the free press under his strict control. He made it illegal to listen to foreign broadcasts – most especially the BBC.

What he hadn't reckoned with was that Norwegians are an extremely tough breed, independently minded and passionate about all things Norwegian. So, they tuned in whenever they could and then passed on the news by word of mouth and in chain letters.

The German response was to order all radios to be confiscated. It had little effect. The Norwegians merely began printing newsletters.

Individuals would print a dozen or so copies of each newsletter and then distribute them. The recipients would then type out and copy more copies and pass those on. In this way the newsletters were soon being read nationwide.

Every niche of life as a Norwegian was tainted. German soldiers even took the school milk intended for low-age children.

Yosef Terboven, the new commander, ruthlessly installed a puppet government and banned all the nation's political parties.

His plan was to pressure people into adopting Nazi principles by infiltrating the country's 50 or so professional associations, not least because almost everybody in Norway belonged to one.

Norwegians always joke that if you have two of them together, you have a conversation; put three of them together and you get an association

Next, the Nazi government attacked the Lutheran Church, demanding that priests discard their vows and reveal what churchgoers told them at confession. Should the priests decline, they were told, they would be sentenced to hard labour.

When Bishops protested, Terboven showed his true colours by nominating puppet bishops. From then on, Norwegians churches were devoid of Norwegians. They worshipped with their priests secretly in private homes and other locations.

Sport was the next to come under attack. Sports clubs and football and ice hockey clubs were similarly dispensed with in favour of puppet teams. The Norwegian reaction was again one of defiance.

When the Germans established a national football league, the Norwegians simply boycotted it and no doubt chuckled to themselves when they discovered that only 27 people turned up to watch the 1942 Cup Final.

Despite Terboven's attempts to 'nazify' the country, he faced not just an uphill battle but an almost vertical one. By May 1943, more than 40 different organisations representing more than 250,000 people had protested, often facing imprisonment or maltreatment in the process.

There were mass arrests and many organisations were banned or put under the control of the Nazis or Quislings.

Again. the Norwegian response was simple and effective; They simply resigned *en masse,* leaving the official associations with no reason to exist.

Meanwhile, their members continued to meet as before, but underground like the priests and bishops.

It is often claimed that Catholics believe that if you 'give me the child, I will give you the man'. The Germans similarly believed that the most effective way of achieving their goals and establishing Nazi ideology would be by reaching out to schoolchildren.

Quisling, the leader of the Norwegian Nazi Party, decreed that all textbooks should be revised to reflect Nazi ideals.

English language schoolbooks were outlawed. German, not English, would now become Norway's second language and every child in the country was required to learn it.

Teachers were horrified and outraged by this assault on human rights, but their choice was simple: submit, or lose their jobs and pensions. They opted instead for mass action.

Quisling was informed individually by each one of nearly 14,000 teachers that they would not go along with his demands, no matter what.

Each letter was identical. The date of postage on the envelopes was the same day for all of them.

Days later, the teachers were backed up by the clergy with priests throughout the country reading out a declaration condemning the attempt to ram Nazi ideals down the throat of education.

Quisling had no option but to admit defeat, but the price was high. More than 1,300 teachers were arrested and most of them ended up being transported to a concentration camp outside Oslo.

Some 700 were bundled into railway cattle trucks and sent to a transition camp where they were severely maltreated, denied proper food and subjected to physical and mental abuse.

Worse was to come. Even teachers suffering from pneumonia, chest and stomach complaints, internal bleeding and nervous breakdowns were among the many who were forced into hard labour in Narvik, in the arctic north of Norway.

Despite the harsh winter weather, the teachers were marched each day to the docks and forced to load and unload supply ships. Each day, local people wore their paperclips and stood silently to watch and show their respect for them.

Such was the teachers' fortitude, that they became legendary throughout Norway and when the war ended, they returned home to be welcomed and celebrated as heroes.

The treatment dished out by the Germans hardened Norwegian attitudes. Now, it was not just a case of ridiculing them. People hated and detested them – sentiments that still exist amongst many Norwegians even today.

As a result, what had been mere unspoken defiance and civil disobedience gradually developed into a strong, highly co-ordinated underground network of resistance. Resistance workers, as they became known, created a secret world of escape routes, safe houses and hiding places for anyone being sought by the Germans.

Thousands of Norwegians contributed their savings and a percentage of their earnings to support the families of men and women who had lost their jobs or pensions, or who had been deported to Germany and imprisoned or executed for what in many cases were minor annoyances or misdemeanours.

This silent insurrection continued despite the risks. On one occasion, resistance workers burned the country's population records in an 'accidental on purpose' fire. On others, they deliberately sabotaged German communications and directives to the public.

The non-violent resistance movement of the early days evolved almost imperceptibly into a nationwide organisation that was much more hard-nosed and active. It ultimately became known simply as 'The Norwegian Resistance' and it was called 'Milorg'.

Some of Milorg's members sailed to Britain in small boats to join the conventional free Norwegian forces.

Others were recruited by the Special Operations Executive (SOE) and the Secret Intelligence Service, (SIS), who trained them to be radio spies.

Their task was to set up radio stations along the Norwegian coast and to send intelligence back to Britain.

Thanks to the fjords and mountains, and often isolated coast, fishing boats were able to slip in and out of occupied Norway with relative ease.

The actual crossings from Norway to Scalloway in the Shetland Islands and back, however, were never easy and always fraught with danger. The fishing boats operated in all weathers almost every week for five years.

Storms and German air attacks took the lives of many men. Despite the risks, Norwegian agents and Resistance workers sailed their fishing boats back and forth so often that they eventually became known as the 'Shetland Bus'.

None of the Norwegian agents were under any illusions about the risks they were running. As one of them said: "If anyone was hurt, *we* would shoot him. Just think what would happen to any one of us being caught!"

As the number of radio spies increased, so did the number of ports and fjords being watched.

Whenever a German convoy was about to leave, agents would transmit the news straight back to Britain and shortly afterwards Royal Air Force bombers would appear on the scene.

In May 1941, a station codenamed Skylark B reported the arrival of three German destroyers at Trondheim.

The RAF knew that the battleship *Bismark* had left the Baltic and sailed into the North Sea with the cruiser *Prins Eugene (pronounced Oi-gen)* and a destroyer escort, but bad weather meant that the pilots had lost contact with them.

Now, the Norwegian Resistance workers had found them again. The Admiralty deployed the Home Fleet and Germany's most powerful warship of the time was located and sunk.

Initially, though, Milorg took a cautious and reluctant approach to sabotage. They didn't think it was worth attracting reprisals against the civilian population.

When British commandoes raided the Lofoten islands in March 1941, Milorg agents were furious, as was the Norwegian government in exile, because the German response was to set fire to dozens of houses and send 70 prominent local people to a prison camp.

Although Britain had withdrawn her troops from Norway in 1940, Germany's invasion of the Soviet Union in June 1941 suddenly and dramatically increased Norway's importance.

Within weeks, Britain was sending supplies to Russia, but German air and naval attacks from Norwegian shores were a constant threat to these "Arctic convoys" as they would famously become known.

Churchill wanted to deal with the problem by invading Norway, although his Chiefs of Staff were reluctant to do so.

Hitler, too, believed that Britain might invade. Indeed, he became *convinced* of it and ordered the Norwegian garrison to be reinforced until there were some 350,000 German troops in the country.

As the number of German troops increased, so too did the activities of Milorg and the number of Norwegian spies entering the country on the Shetland bus.

They were preoccupied with tracking the German battleship *Tirpitz* and other German ships, which constituted a major threat to the Russian convoys.

Eventually, there were radio stations along Norway's entire coastline and some radio spies ran incredible risks trying to install radio stations, even in restricted German zones.

In an interview with Norwegian State Television, NRK, a former 'H7' agent Bjørn Raaholt made light of his extraordinary courage and sheer brazenness in dealing with the Germans.

"I was fitted out as an insurance salesman with false papers, (and) the only correct thing about it was that it said 'agent' on it," he recalled.

"I simply took the coastal steamer and walked off the steamer and up to the Kommandant's office and I explained to him that I had arrived from Oslo that morning on the night train and I simply did not have time to get the special papers which were necessary for me to be permitted to enter the fortress – and here are my credentials and would he please give his personal permission for me to go around and see my Norwegian clients.

"And he jokingly asked me if I wanted to make an insurance policy for him and I told him that, no, as a matter of principle, we never take risks on German naval officers and he thought this was a huge joke and he gave me his permission.

"We then parted and I went to see a very brave man, Magna Hassle, who had promised to operate the transmitter".

Thanks to such men, the German ships were under constant surveillance for three years, with reports going back to Britain every time they weighed anchor.

But the Germans were beginning to crack down on the Resistance. Olof Reid Olsson had a very lucky

escape.

Just hours after this photograph was taken, he and his fellow agents found themselves fleeing for their lives.

"All round the district they (German troops) had circled the whole thing with close to 600 men and we ran from one machine gun post into another one constantly," he recounted.

"And, of course, they started firing like mad and then we had these running patrols after us, and if we didn't have the physical fitness that we did have then, of course, we would never make it.

"As I always said to the boys: 'We are the boss. No Germans can outwit us when it comes to the woods'.

"Well, the Germans and the police cars were running all the time up and down the valley, so we took the ordinary bus in to town.

"Went through two controls, had our papers and nobody said a word. So, by doing what they didn't think we would do certainly saved us that time."

The Norwegian spies were now under extreme pressure and in ever greater danger.

The Gestapo launched a major crackdown on Milorg and managed to infiltrate the ranks of informers, who together with many agents, were imprisoned or executed at the whim of local Nazi commanders.

By early 1942, Milorg in southern Norway at least had all but ceased to exist – and constant searches and counter-measures elsewhere threatened to crush the activities of the radio spies.

It was precisely at this time, when it seemed that Milorg was on its knees, that the allies became aware of another threat.

This was a menace so great that one Norwegian resistance worker recalled being told that if the Germans succeeded in their endeavours, they would have the capacity to blow up the whole of London.

That terrible thought was the opening paragraph, if you like, of one of the greatest feats of resistance in the history of warfare.

I refer, of course, to the story of heavy water production at the Vermork power station, near Ryukan, some 70 miles or so west of Oslo in the Telemark district of Norway.

The reader may remember the famous Hollywood film directed by Anthony Mann in 1965 entitled *"The*

Heroes of Telemark" starring Kirk Douglas and Richard Harris. That was a good yarn, but this is the real story:

Heavy water, incidentally, is simply ordinary water in which the two hydrogen atoms, as in H2O, have been replaced with deuterium atoms, making it D2O, which is about ten per cent heavier.

That process of electrolysis also means that people like Hitler can make an atomic bomb using plutonium, thus entirely by-passing the need to enrich uranium.

However, the process of producing heavy water is very slow and similar to the distillation of alcohol, just a few drops at a time.

Nonetheless, Norsk Hydro, the company running the power plant, was producing 100 kilos of heavy water a month.

The Germans demanded an immediate increase in production – because without heavy water, they had no hope at all of making an atom bomb during the course of the war.

Norsk Hydro's management protested. The Germans responded by sending the Managing Director, Bjarne Eriksen, to a concentration camp in Germany.

When Norwegian spies informed London of all this, British Intelligence realised they would have to get somebody inside the factory quickly to find out exactly what was going on.

In addition, that somebody would have to be a resistance worker who not only knew the plant, but who

had the necessary technical qualifications to be able to monitor the situation properly. It seemed a very tall order indeed.

Then, by pure chance, a man called Einar Skinnerland escaped to Britain.

When British Intelligence vetted him, he told them that he not only lived close to the

Norsk Hydro plant at Rjukan, but that he was also a hydroelectric technician.

It was an extraordinary piece of luck, a gift from heaven!

What's more, it turned out that Skinnerland was also an expert skier and to top it all an amateur radio operator, as well. Clearly, he was the ideal man for the job.

In the early hours of the 29th of March, 1942, Skinnerland parachuted onto the vast expanse of mountain snows to the northwest of Rjukan in bitterly cold weather. Having gradually made his way to the town, he then managed to get a job with a construction team at the heavy water plant.

It did not take him very long to establish that if the British were to thwart Hitler's nuclear plans, they could not afford to waste time in halting the production of heavy water.

So, on October the 19th, 1942, the British launched 'Operation Grouse'.

It called for a team of four Norwegian commandos, specially trained by the SOE and codenamed the 'Swallows' to be parachuted into the mountain wilderness of Telemark.

Their job was to establish a *route* to the plant and to guide a second team – British paratrooper engineers who would fly to Norway in gliders.

Unfortunately, the RAF dropped the 'Swallows' at the wrong place and, as a result, the team took a very long time to ski to Rjukan, hiding in the daytime and travelling at night.

In fact, it took so long that British Intelligence began to suspect that they had been captured. However, the 'Swallows' did reach Rjukan and when they were finally able to contact the British, the SOE were suspicious. They asked a coded question: "What did you see in the early morning of such-and-such a day". When the 'Swallows' gave the pre-arranged reply: "Three pink elephants", the British were ecstatic.

In the meantime, Einar Skinnerland had warned the British that the Germans had recently brought in strong reinforcements to the guard at the heavy water plant.

Nonetheless, with the 'Swallows' now in place, the British decided to go ahead with the next phase of the operation. It was known as 'Operation Freshman' and it turned out to be a disaster.

On the 19th of November, 1942, two large gliders towed by Halifax bombers took off from Wick in northeast Scotland.

On board each of the gliders were two pilots and 15 Royal Engineers of the First British Airborne Division.

Unfortunately, they ran into bad weather and all the aircraft crashed, with many dead and injured.

The Germans eventually caught the survivors and the Gestapo even tortured the badly injured. Later, they executed them all. Not until after the war were their bodies exhumed and full details of the murder were revealed.

The Norwegian 'Swallows', meanwhile, went to ground up in the mountains. They were short of food and now had to wait until another attempt could be mounted.

For three months, they managed to avoid detection but, as one of them, Klaus Hellberg, recalled, it wasn't easy.

"We hadn't much food left so we were anxious", he said. "I remember we started digging into the snow to get moss." But, as luck would have it, moss and lichen were not on the menu for long. Just before Christmas, they managed to bag a reindeer.

The British began planning another attempt, codenamed Operation Gunnerside – which was named after the moorland where Sir Charles Hambro, the head of the SOE, used to shoot grouse.

The SOE chose a seasoned Norwegian officer, Lt. Joakkim Rønneberg, to lead it. "I was told we were going to Vermork, to blow up this heavy water factory and we were also told about the little group of

Norwegians who had been back in Norway as a reception committee," he said.

Rønneberg and five other Norwegians, all superb skiers, trained and rehearsed the raid in Scotland using detailed plans provided by the Resistance.

Their first attempt on the 23rd of January, 1943, failed because the bomber crew were unable to find the lights set out by the 'Swallows' to mark the parachute drop zone.

So, the Gunnerside team had to wait for the next full moon. They parachuted onto the Hardanger plateau northwest of Rjukan on the 16th February, 1943, but strong winds drove them a long way from the drop zone and it was several days before they were able to link up with the 'Swallows'.

"I'll never forget that meeting", Rønneberg recalled to an NRK intervuer. "Oj oj...marvellous. I heard someone shouting 'Hello'. And that was one of the men and we were of course very, very happy. And then we saw the others. They were... they had been hiding..."

The combined team made final preparations for the assault, planned for the 27th February. The only way to reach the Norsk Hydro plant was across a single, 246-foot (75-metre) long bridge, which was 650 feet (200 metres) above the river.

German sentries were posted at each end of it. They had planted mines, set up floodlights and posted additional guards around the plant.

During the winter months, however, security had become lax, the Germans convinced that the steep sides of the gorge were impassable.

One of the team went to investigate and found that,

despite being very steep, the gorge was climbable. He then returned to the hut and the group debated the choice – bridge or gorge.

"We voted about it and I think five or six were for the gorge", one of them said. "and the others for the bridge. Two officers, they were for the bridge. But we decided to use the gorge. We started about eight o clock in the evening. It was dark. We crossed the gorge with our weapons and the munitions".

It took them nearly four hours to reach the perimeter fence and to their surprise there seemed to be no sentries around. After cutting the single chain and padlock without difficulty and using detailed plans provided by Einar Skinnerland, who was still working at the plant, they eventually entered the basement through a cable tunnel and a window without alerting the guards.

The only person they came across was a Norwegian caretaker called Johansen, who was more than willing to help them.

As they entered the electrolysis hall, the caretaker said he had lost his spectacles. Realising that it would have been almost impossible to buy new ones at the time, some of the agents made a frantic search for them.

Happily, they found them and the other agents were able to lay the charges and light the two-minute fuses.

The saboteurs deliberately left behind a British submachine gun to suggest that local resistance was not involved – and hopefully alleviate German reprisals.

The heavy water cells and the storage tanks were completely destroyed, putting the plant out of action for several months.

Even General Nicholaus von Falkenhorst, the German military commander in Norway, admitted that it had been a spectacular operation. He ordered thousands of men to scour the region, but all ten commandos escaped. Six of them skied 240 miles (400 kilometres) to Sweden.

The other four, including Klaus Hellberg, stayed in Norway and continued to work with the resistance.

A few weeks later, as he skied towards one of the safe houses, he suddenly found himself ski-ing for his life:

"I was relaxed. I was glad to be by myself. Good skiing conditions. When I got there, I saw lots of ski tracks outside the huts. And I was suspicious. Why are there so many ski tracks? Then from the hut, I saw Germans, that Germans had discovered this particular hut.

"I climbed as fast as I possibly could into my skis and ran off. Then the Germans started shooting. Shouting and shooting. I thought this is the end. Two men managed to keep up and chase me. After a while there was only one.

"The only thing I thought was: you have to be faster. Even faster to get away. When I was skiing uphill, I was faster. When skiing downhill, he was faster. In the long downhill, he was quite close to me. I took my pistol out and shot two shots. I didn't hit. And he started shooting at me. He didn't hit me.

"And... er, when he had no more shots, he turned as quickly as he could. I sent him two shots and he ran away."

By April, 1943, the Germans had repaired the plant and heavy water production resumed. The SOE knew that with massive security, a repeat commando raid was all but impossible.

So, in November 1943, more than 140 B-17 bombers dropped 711 bombs. At least 600 missed their target, but the electrolysis plant was destroyed and, now, the Germans had had enough.

They decided to halt heavy water production in Norway – and ship the remaining stocks and critical components back to Germany.

In London, Einar Skinnerland's information left no doubt as to what must be done. The train and ferry shipments *had* to be stopped.

Knut Haukelid, one of the Norsk Hydro team who stayed behind in Norway to help the Resistance with more raids led the operation. Despite the risk of what we now call collateral damage, in other words, civilian deaths, King Haak*on* himself approved the operation.

"And it ended up with a definite order to do it," Haukelid told NRK. "I know for certain it was taken up in the Norwegian cabinet meeting. And the order was to sink it at any cost."

The heavy water first had to be moved from the plant at Rjukan by railway and from there onto a ferry at Lake Tinnsjø before resuming its journey to Oslo. Unfortunately, the train and the track were swarming with German guards. Any attempt at sabotage would be a suicide mission.

On the evening of February the 19th, the wagons were shunted into sidings. German troops patrolled the area continuously. But they failed to guard the ferry.

"We just walked onto the ferry in the middle of the night, got around the Norwegian watchman who was there, went down to the bilges and laid a delayed charge which would sink the ferry," Haukelid added.

Just after midnight, the wagons were shunted on board as two 'alarm-clock' fuses ticked away next to nearly 19 lbs (8½ kilos) of plastic explosive.

The ferry set sail and when the explosives detonated, it sank in the deepest part of the lake within five minutes, taking Hitler's dream of an atomic bomb with it.

The Norwegian Resistance continued to harass the Germans until the end of the war. One of its more imaginative efforts was to contaminate fish bound for Germany, poisoning scores of Germans.

The efforts of the radio spies enabled the British finally to sink the battleships *Scharnhorst* and *Tirpitz*. Norwegian torpedo boats based at Lerwick in the Shetland Islands repeatedly crossed the North Sea, hid in deep fjords and attacked German shipping.

Milorg increased its sabotage attacks, tying down 350,000 German troops that might otherwise have been active in central Europe.

Hitler remained to the end convinced that Britain would invade Norway and, as the date for the Normandy invasion approached, Churchill was determined to keep him thinking that way.

Radio trucks toured the Scottish Highlands broadcasting fake radio traffic to a fictitious army supposedly preparing to land in Norway.

The radio spies also played a vital role in providing weather reports. They all thought it immensely boring, but when Atlantic storms delayed the D-Day landings for 24 hours, it was they who predicted a lull in the weather – allowing General Eisenhower to give the go-ahead for the landings.

In May, 1945, a single representative of Milorg's 60,000 members took the surrender of 350,000 German troops.

The S.S. commander in Norway, Wilhelm Rediess, shot himself and the German Reichskommander, Yosef Terboven, blew himself up with 110lbs (50 kilos) of dynamite. He obviously didn't want to make any mistakes!

Norwegian authorities interned thousands of Nazi party members in the same concentration camp in which the Norwegian teachers had been imprisoned.

The camp was overcrowded and poorly supplied. Understandably, perhaps, the Norwegian guards treated the prisoners brutally. Approximately 18,000 people were imprisoned for war crimes and 25 collaborators and 12 Germans were executed, as indeed was Vidkun Quisling, the leader of Norway's Nazi party.

It took many, many years for the hatred to cool and the trauma to ease. Even today, the scars still exist.

When the Nazis retreated, they razed town after town to the ground. There are very few towns, in northern Norway, particularly with any buildings preceding 1945.

In Molde, on the west coast, only three buildings in the entire town survived.

The Germans never did catch on to the significance of Norwegian civilians wearing paper clips in their lapels. For they were, very simply, badges of resistance against oppression, and symbols of pride in their country.

***

Westward with the Vikings

Some years ago, when I was working as a television news reporter, I was fortunate (or perhaps unfortunate) enough to be assigned to take a cruise across the North Sea.

It was unfortunate because the ship nearly sank. Fortunate because it launched me onto a learning curve about those fascinating seafarers – the Vikings, who, a thousand years ago, sailed in sturdy, ocean-going boats to North America.

It has always been assumed that the Viking Age began with the raid on Lindisfarne in 793 AD – but that date is a mere historical convenience. Ocean-going boats suggest otherwise.

For instance, one Iron Age boat, albeit with no keel but still capable of carrying 22 people, was found in Jutland, Denmark dating back to 350 BC.

Boats with dragonheads were sailing around the islands along the west Norwegian coast as early as 500 BC and the so-called *Kvalsund* ship was 59 feet (18 metres) long with an oak keel and pine frames dating back to 690 AD.

It, too, was capable of carrying 22 men with their supplies and weapons.

So, the Vikings who sailed to Scotland, Ireland, Iceland, Greenland and North America in the late 10th century had nearly 1,000 years of boatbuilding expertise upon which they could draw!

Of course, the Vikings have a fearsome reputation. But they were no worse than rival Irish groups who plundered and burned each other's monasteries with considerable enthusiasm.

The Moors from Spain and the Magyars from Hungary also undertook brutal military expeditions and whilst historians portrayed the Vikings as being exceptionally bloodthirsty and cruel, they failed to mention that the Christians were equally ferocious, plundering and killing each other, and others, with alacrity.

Arguably, the Vikings gave as much to society as they ever took from it, so let us look at some of the Viking achievements; at their ships and how they built them, how they navigated them and more importantly how they survived after sailing well beyond what a thousand years ago was the very edge of the known world.

Let us embark on our own voyage of discovery and journey westward with the Vikings.

The ship in the photograph on the next page is of the most authentic replica of a Viking ship that has ever been built.

This is her story – and to some extent, mine too.

My own interest in the Vikings was sparked off some years ago, when I was an on-screen reporter for *News at Ten*.

I walked into the newsroom one breezy Saturday morning to be greeted by the duty Foreign Editor, who said: "Don't take your coat off. How do you fancy a cruise across the North Sea?"

My face lit up. "Fantastic," I said. "Anything's better than sitting around the office all weekend."

"All right," he said. "I want you to fly to Stavanger in Norway. You'll be there this evening. Ship leaves tomorrow morning. With a bit of luck, you'll be back by Friday."

I was delighted, but then I thought: "Friday? That's six days! What kind of ship is it," I asked, "that takes six days across the North Sea?"

"Ah!" said the Foreign Editor. "Thought you'd ask that. Actually, it's an open Viking ship and you'll be the first to cross the North Sea in one of those for 900 years, mate."

So, I flew to Stavanger for my cruise!

On arrival, I gazed down on a "ship" which, to me, seemed not much bigger than a lifeboat and I must confess that I was a little apprehensive.

Nor was my concern alleviated when two extremely hairy individuals greeted me on the quayside. Individuals who looked for the entire world like the traditional image of their ancestors.

Ragnar Thorseth   Trygve Berge

Happily, I was I good hands because a couple of years earlier, in 1981, Ragnar Thorseth, on the left, and Trygve Berge, the cameraman who took most of the pictures in this chapter of the book, had sailed through the North West Passage – in a cabin cruiser.

It turned out that they were the first to complete that voyage since Roald Amundsen 75 years earlier.

Not satisfied with that, in 1982, they became the first Norwegians to reach the North Pole, something not even Nansen or Amundsen had been able to achieve.

It was during that North Pole expedition that Thorseth and Berge hit on the idea of sailing from Norway to Iceland, Greenland and North America in the wake of the Viking chieftain, Erik the Red, and his son, Leif Eriksson.

Erik had settled in Greenland in 982 AD, and his son Leif Eriksson had lived in North America several centuries before the birth of Columbus, who, so far as I've been able to establish, neither discovered nor actually set foot in America. What Columbus did find was Haiti – and he thought it was China!

Thanks to a renowned Norwegian archaeologist, Dr. Helge Ingstad and his wife, Anne Stina, we now know that Leif Eriksson reached a tiny settlement called L'Anse aux Meadows on the northern tip of Newfoundland.

Here, the Ingstads found the ruins of several houses, including a long house with a central hearth. They also found stones cracked by fire and ember pits filled with charcoal.

These were well-known features in Viking houses discovered previously in Greenland and Iceland. To begin with, only the Ingstads believed that this was indeed a Norse settlement.

In an interview with Norwegian State Television, NRK, Dr. Ingstad described the ruined houses they had found:

"Personally, I had a strong feeling that this must be Norse. They lay there so beautiful on the hill and it reminded me so much of about homes I had seen in western Norway and in Greenland. So, I said to myself exactly such a place Norse people would select for their homesteads."

Ingstad's wife, Anne Stine, picked up the story: "In the course of the excavation, the first year in the fall, I was pretty sure that it was a Norse settlement, but of course we had to persuade people about it and that took about eight years."

During those eight years, the husband and wife team also found bog iron, a piece of bronze, some charcoal and a stone anvil.

These were highly significant because neither the Inuit people (formerly known as Eskimos) nor the Indians were capable of working metal.

So, the people who had lived in the houses were definitely from foreign shores. Moreover, a Carbon-14 test dated this material to the eleventh century, precisely the time of the Viking expansion westwards.

Yet, the Ingstad's discoveries were still treated with great scepticism.

Can you imagine how they felt? After eight years of effort and knowing in their bones that they were right, not least because the Icelandic Sagas – Erik's Saga and the Saga of the Greenlanders.

These tell us in great detail how one Bjarni Herjolfsson was sailing to Greenland and was caught in a storm and blown southwest, past Greenland and there sighted unknown lands.

The Sagas go on to relate how, 15 years later, Leif Eriksson set out to find the land of which Bjarni had spoken.

What Leif and his crew found has intrigued historians ever since. He called the new land 'Vinland'.

The Sagas describe a land of rolling grasslands, meadows with wild wheat, forests in which there was an abundance of game and rivers teeming with salmon.

Furthermore, the Sagas, or at least one interpretation of them, speak of frost-free winters and summer countryside filled with wild grapes, and it has always been assumed that wine made from those grapes gave Vinland its name.

Happily, the Ingstads eventually won the recognition they deserved because in 1961, they unearthed a bronze pin and a spindle whorl that were indisputably of Norse origin. These, together with other finds, proved that the Vikings, not Columbus, were the

the first foreigners to settle in North America.

Recently, scientists have discovered what is almost certainly a second Viking site in North America, at Port Rosee, 400 miles southwest of L'Anse aux Meadows.

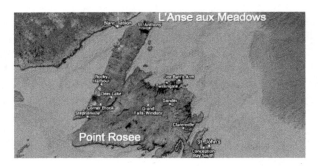

High resolution imagery from satellites orbiting nearly 500 miles above the earth, combined with infrared technology captured the outlines of a building similar to a longhouse.

Excavations at the site have unearthed the head of an iron nail dating to between 800 and 1,300AD, again, precisely the time of the Viking Expansion westwards.

The Viking voyages west had been carried out in short stages over the best part of a century. From Norway, they first sailed to the Shetland, Orkney and Faroe Islands, and from there to the west coast of Britain and Ireland, and on to Iceland.

From Iceland to Cape Farewell at the southern tip of Greenland took four days in fair weather.

Later, they sailed north, along Greenland's west coast to what is now the country's capital, Nuuk. From there they crossed the Davis Strait to explore Baffin Island and Labrador, and then followed the coast down to L'Anse aux Meadows in Newfoundland *(see map p.104)*.

There, they established a small settlement or possibly just a transit camp.

All this took place over a century or so, but it is very difficult to imagine that once men with such a tradition of exploration had built permanent structures at L'Anse aux Meadows, they would not sail further down the coast to New England or beyond simply to see what was there!

This had a deep impact on Ragnar Thorseth, but it was in Denmark that his imagination was really fired. Here, in the mud of the Roskilde fjord to the west of Copenhagen, marine archaeologists had discovered no fewer than five Viking ships.

Vikings had sunk them deliberately some 900 years earlier to form a barrier across the fjord and thus protect from enemy fleets the important trading centre of Roskilde, which was also a burial place for Danish Royalty. They were known as the Skuldelev ships.

There was a long ship, a warship, a small ferry or fishing boat, a coastal vessel and a large, ocean-going trader known as a *knarr*.

It was in a *knarr* that Erik the Red had sailed to Greenland and Leif Eriksson to L'Anse aux Meadows in Newfoundland. Indeed, the *knarr* enabled the Vikings to cross the north Atlantic regularly for 500 years.

 Until this time, the common perception of a Viking ship was based on two vessels in the Viking Ship Museum in Oslo.

The first was the Oseberg ship, noted for the exquisite carvings on her prow, and here we begin to see what the Vikings gave to society.

Yet these carvings, combined with her general unseaworthiness, suggest that Oseberg was used only in calm waters for ceremonial purposes, and finally as a burial ship.

A more robust ship was required by Vikings raiding Scotland, Ireland, England and France. They used the Gokstad ship.

This was a war machine, almost devoid of decoration, 76 feet (23 metres) long. It was capable of carrying 70 men and four tons of weaponry, food, water and other cargo

Thanks to her shallow draft, the Viking raiders could slip quietly into an inlet, beach the ship, take unsuspecting monks by surprise, then steal their silver and other treasures, and sail away again before anyone could raise an army to thwart them.

In fact, it was it was the *knarr*, the deep-sea trading ship, that was the backbone of the Viking fleet and the *knarr* found at Skuldelev in the Roskilde fjord was the first, indeed the only *knarr*, ever found.

But the problem with wrecks is that they tell us very little, if anything, about the size of the mast or the sail. Or about how the ships were rigged. Or how they behaved at sea.

Ragnar Thorseth's planned voyage across the Atlantic provided the ideal opportunity to find out!

As more than 60 per cent of her had been recovered and reassembled, it gave Ragnar Thorseth and the museum experts the first opportunity to see exactly how the Vikings built such ships.

He knew precisely who should build the *knarr*. And the artisan most qualified was Sigurd Bjorkedal, whose family have passed on the tradition of boatbuilding from

at least the 16th century

Sigurd Bjørkedal, master shipbuilder.

In Bjorkedalen, the valley named after the family, the boatbuilding tradition goes right back to Viking times and, in June 1982, Sigurd Bjorkedal and his sons felled the first trees for this new project.

Next, they stripped them of their bark and left them to age before beginning construction. In order to save time, Bjorkedal opted to compromise his normal preparatory methods and decided instead to cut the planking with a circular saw, which was much quicker than using axes.

However, this meant a slight reduction in the strength of the planking because the saw blade does not follow the natural grain of the wood, as would an axe when splitting them by hand.

Usually, Bjorkedal followed traditional methods handed down through the centuries but experts at the Roskilde Viking Ship Museum had prepared detailed diagrams of the wreck and they were keen that he should use them.

They wanted every detail to be exactly the same as in the original *knarr*, right down to the last centimetre. Bjørkedal, however, had great faith in his ability to measure simply with his own eyes!

Once he had laid the oak keel, which in this case measured 46 feet (14 metres), the keel **board** was attached with a wooden vice and then nailed into place with iron spikes, which, incidentally, the Norsemen first began to use in their ships 300 years before Christ.

One cannot help but marvel at the incredible accuracy that a master ship-builder can achieve simply by using his own eyes.

The ribs were notched with an axe so that they would fit each individual, clinker-built plank.

When the ribs were in place, they were fastened to the planks with wooden pins driven in from the bottom and then locked into place with wooden wedges driven in from the top.

The mast-foot is traditionally fashioned from a single tree trunk, with part of a branch running off about one third of the way up.

The mast-foot is vitally important because it supports the entire weight of the mast, sail and rig. And since it fits over each rib individually), it also adds strength to the basic structure of the ship.

During the building process, experts from the museum visited the site on several occasions and from time to time there were differences between the drawings, (in other words how the experts believed the ship should be constructed on the basis of what they had found in the mud) and the traditions handed down from father to son through the centuries.

The drawings dictated that the ship's circumference should be exactly 12 metres, about 40 feet, but while Sigurd Bjorkedal frequently referred to the drawings, he had in fact relied much more on his own eyes.

Remarkably, when he and his sons had completed the ship, they were less than one centimetre out. That's the width of a little fingernail.

From now on, though, it would all be guesswork. The only reference as to how a Viking ship was rigged was the Bayeaux tapestry. No-one knew how tall the mast should be or how large the sail.

That said, Thorseth and his helpers were not working completely blind. Norwegians had after all been building boats for nearly two thousand years and there were many known boatbuilding techniques upon which they could draw.

One method, dating back centuries, was to use a willow sapling to attach the steering oar to the side of the ship.

These saplings are very difficult to work with and the crew were not certain how to cure them properly. So, they opted to soak them in boiling tar together with 1,800 metres or more than a mile of hemp rope for the rigging

Next, the willow sapling was threaded through the steering oar and then pulled through an opening in the side of the ship.

This doesn't look particularly strong, but I was assured that the Vikings would have used just such a method and that it had served them well. The boiled willow was then tied securely, a distinctly messy business. After that, all that remained was to see if it worked.

Experts estimated that the new ship would require approximately 1,000 square feet (93 square metres) of sail. The mast itself would be 13 metres or 43 feet tall, with a diameter of 32 centimetres, about twelve-and-a-half inches.

A replica Viking coin was chosen as the ship's lucky charm and placed beneath the mast. The Vikings, of course, did not have a modern crane to help raise the mast.

So, instead, they would find a suitable cliff and with a considerable amount of manpower, much huffing and puffing, yet more rope and a simple block and tackle, they could finally raise the mast into position.

In Viking times, the forests were much more extensive in Norway than they are today and while this was helpful in terms of easy access to timber for building houses and ships, it also meant that as the population grew, there was an acute shortage of agricultural land.

If a Viking farmer died, his eldest son inherited the farm. The second and third sons thus had no hope of ever owning their own farms.

And if a Viking youth wanted to marry, he had to pay the girl's father a house bond (the origin of the word husband). If he had no farm, he certainly wouldn't be able to afford such a bond and therefore couldn't marry.

So, it was for these reasons that the Vikings became such feared raiders. Plunder from foreign shores enabled them to marry and eventually live comfortable farming lives.

This acute shortage of land was the main reason for Vikings settling abroad and in almost every instance, they quickly integrated with the local population.

In fact, the Vikings never had ambitions to establish a Viking empire.

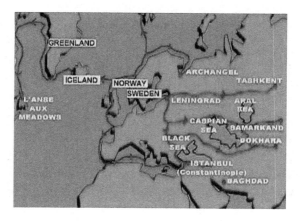

Nonetheless, apart from their journeys to Iceland, Greenland and North America, the Vikings sailed to France, Spain, Portugal and the Mediterranean.

Swedish Vikings sailed across the Baltic and struck deep into Germany and Poland, along the great Russian river routes south to the Black Sea and Constantinople.

Often hauling their ships overland from one river to another, they eventually traded with merchants from Persia in Bagdad, and from China in the great trading cities of Tashkent, Samarkand and Bokhara to the east, the source of their most prized commodities.

The prize for these tortuous journeys was silver and some gold. More than 60,000 Arab coins have been found in Scandinavia. The Vikings often treated these as bullion and frequently melted them down to make jewellery or to use for ornamental purposes.

Such is the artistry and craftsmanship of their gold-and-silversmiths that their designs have been handed down through the centuries and are still being reproduced and sold today.

With well over a thousand silver hoards discovered, we are left in no doubt as to the Viking's ability to accumulate wealth, by fair means or foul.

This wagon is the only complete wheeled vehicle preserved from the Viking Age. It was probably made to carry a wealthy Viking woman.

The body of the wagon was removable and bearded figures on each corner acted as hooks with which to anchor the ropes.

Meanwhile, back in the twentieth century, Ragnar Thorseth's Viking *knarr* was about to be christened with a horn of mead by none other than the archaeologist, Anna Stina Ingstad. They named the ship Saga *Siglar*, Sailor of the Sagas!

But during sea trials, fears about the strength of the willow sapling holding the steering oar in place proved well founded. Ninety miles out into the North Sea, the sapling snapped and we floundered helplessly while the oar was dragged on board for repair.

Later that night, as the weather deteriorated into a Force Seven wind, the oar itself broke and we spent more than an hour trying to get a line across to our support ship so that we could be towed back to Norway. Nor was the steering oar our only problem.

The wooden rope tighteners were also proving unsatisfactory with the result that the rigging rapidly became loose and, much more dangerous, the mast began to sway alarmingly from side to side.

The danger, of course, was that the strain would cause the mast to break or, much worse, that it would sway so much as to keel the boat over.

Ragnar Thorseth admitted at this stage that the mast was too small for the sail.

I must admit that I could not help but think of the landlubber who observed on his first voyage that there was "an awful lot of sea", to which an old sailor replied: "Certainly is, and that's just the top of it."

While the eight-strong crew battled with the steering oar, I made my feelings known in a standupper (which is when a reporter speaks to the camera and thus the nation at large) in which I said:

"Sometimes, the crew would joke that Erik the Red sailed to Greenland with 25 ships and only 14 of them got there. Now, the joke is wearing a bit thin because here we are in the North Sea without a rudder."

At this stage, the ship suddenly lurched broadside on to a wave and I added: "It's not a very comfortable feeling!"

In retrospect, it was a somewhat inglorious picture of a much younger me secretly cursing ITN's duty foreign editor and wishing fervently that he was back home mowing the lawn!

Of course, as Ragnar Thorseth pointed out, the very purpose of this voyage was to find out how the Vikings rigged their ships and trial and error was the only way to do that. I just wish someone had told me!

In any event, Saga *Siglar* was soon fitted with a new and heavier mast and the ballast was increased from ten to 16 tons.

Perhaps we should also remember that when the Vikings sailed across the Atlantic, they loaded their *knarr*s to the gunnels with provisions, wives and children, timber and seed corn, as well as sheep, goats and horses.

The conditions were often terrible, for these could be among the stormiest seas in the world. Inevitably, some ships were overwhelmed, who knows, perhaps because those willow saplings holding the steering oars in place were not strong enough.

Overall, the Viking *knarrs* with their high, swan-breasted prows, were exceptionally stable and easy to handle.

They were also very fast. They could make 13 knots in good conditions and were probably the fastest boats in the world at the time. Of course, the men who sailed them had no proper compass or lodestone.

They could hold course accurately on a latitude by observing the sun and stars provided they were not obscured by cloud, but they had no failsafe way of calculating longitude.

What they did have was a primitive bearing-dial, a small, notched disc which they used in conjunction with a set of tables showing the height of the midday sun for every week of the year.

This bearing dial was an archaeological find, a wooden plate discovered in 1948 in the colony of Greenland.

Scientists believe the curved line which has been deliberately carved into the plate shows the sun's travel over the sky during a clear day.

The line was created by the shadow from a cone positioned in the middle. A short shadow at noon and a long shadow at dusk.

To use the compass as a directional tool, it had to be turned until the sun's shadow touched the curved line.

The marks around the edges then showed the directions for north, south, east and west.

In one way, the bearing dial was better than a modern compass because at the southern coast of Greenland, a magnetic compass may have shown a deviation of up to 40 degrees.

That simply isn't a problem with a sun compass. It's always correct.

Still, it was by no means perfect. Indeed, I am reminded of the story of two inexperienced sailors struggling through a storm-tossed Atlantic and heading for New York harbour.

One turned from his chart-table and said to the other: "You could at least take your hat off."

"Why's that?" asked his worried shipmate.

"Because according to my calculations," the navigator replied, "we're sailing up the aisle of St. Patrick's Cathedral."

Although the bearing dial was by no means perfect, it did mean that the Vikings could sail into uncharted waters and, more importantly, find their way back again.

Consequently, in the 10th century, the Vikings established the first trading routes across the North Atlantic and sailed those routes on a regular basis for some 500 years.

Unfortunately, they were susceptible to strong crosswinds and many ships were blown off course.

Nonetheless, contrary to previous opinion the voyage of Saga *Siglar* proved that a Viking *knarr* could sail 45 degrees into the wind with only moderate drift.

Happily, most of the ships that set out for Iceland and other destinations did, in fact, arrive safely.

In the meantime, Erik the Red, who had settled in the northwest corner of Iceland, fell into dispute with his neighbours, allowed his temper and his sword to get the better of him and was subsequently declared an outlaw.

In those days, more than 1,000 years ago, the word 'outlaw' meant just that: outside the law and that also implied that anyone could seize an outlaw's property and goods and claim them as their own.

With his enemies hard on his heels and seeking justice, Erik embarked somewhat hurriedly to explore the Greenlandic coast, which had been sighted by storm-swept sailors some years earlier.

Erik liked what he saw and decided to settle there. He called this new land 'Green Land' because he knew that if he was to colonise it, he would have to persuade others to join him and he thought his name for it would make it sound sufficiently attractive.

No doubt if Erik the Red was alive today, he would be working for a major ad agency.

In the summer of 984, Erik returned briefly to Breidafjord in Iceland and then set sail with a fleet of 25 ships carrying several hundred prospective settlers, their ships crammed with livestock and everything they needed to establish a colony in a new land.

As I recounted earlier, only 14 of those ships arrived safely, although it is believed that some of the others did make it back to Iceland.

The southern tip of Greenland was 700 nautical miles away. This was a voyage of four to seven days often in gale force winds and Ragnar Thorseth had already been told to expect the worst ice conditions on record off the east coast of Greenland.

Sure enough, Saga *Siglar* was soon in pack ice drifting south from the polar seas to Cape Farewell, where normally it melts.

Unfortunately, in 1984, the year of Saga Siglar's voyage, the ice completely encircled the coast, and the ship was forced 1000 miles off course and for three days she was out of contact.

Tin those days, the ice here was in constant motion and extended 20 miles from the coast, so for a wooden ship, it was a beautiful, but formidable hazard.

What thoughts would have crossed the minds of the Norsemen who landed here ten centuries ago, I wonder?

Relief, certainly, at having survived the voyage and no doubt curiosity tinged with apprehension, too, because fresh water, good grazing and hopefully no hostile tribes were vital for a successful settlement.

Erik the Red found the fertile grasslands he needed along the fjords of southwestern Greenland.

Here he established his farm on a hill at Bratthalid, overlooking the fjord that until recently bores his name (it is now known by Inuit name, Qassiarsuk).

Extensive excavations show that there were some 200 farms there and that at one stage, the total population of the colony rose to about 5,000.

Agriculturally, the settlers were advanced and excavations have shown that they built artificial lakes and extensive viaduct systems to carry meltwater from the glaciers down to their farms.

To begin with, they lived well. They raised sheep, goats and cattle, as well as pigs and ponies, which they used for herding and for transport.

On the largest farms, there were as many as 100 head of cattle.

The rivers and fjords abounded with fish and the settlers were able to supplement their diet with such larger game as walrus, seals, the occasional polar bear and even the odd whale.

Reindeer and caribou provided meat, hides and utensils from their antlers and bones. Then, incredibly, the 5,000 Norsemen living here simply dwindled away and disappeared.

That is the subject for another chapter in another book (*The Ultimate Cruise Passenger's Guide to Greenland*) but for now, suffice to say it was probably a combination of a sharp decline in trade, a rapid deterioration in climate, conflict with the Inuit and ultimately starvation coupled with disease.

We do know that by 1261, Greenland had succumbed to the political power of Norway and that the King consented to send only one ship every four years.

He also banned all other trade with the Greenlanders, so from 1367, no ships at all visited the settlements.

There were two settlements: one at Bratthalid in the south, where Erik the Red had established his farm, and the other near the present capital, Nuuk, on the west coast of Greenland.

With the advent of a new, mini-Ice Age, the Inuit moved south again, wiped out the western settlement and frequently attacked the farms in the south.

It is not difficult to imagine that as the ice tightened its grip on the coast, hunting became more difficult, sheep and cattle probably died and gradually starvation and disease set in.

What we *do* know is that by the 15th century, these once proud Norsemen had degenerated into a stunted, puny people deformed by malnutrition.

The last record of the Viking community is of a wedding in 1408 and it would be more than 200 years before an outsider set foot in Greenland again.

For Saga *Siglar*, of course, the journey was not yet completed. Bound now for the Viking settlement at L'Anse aux Meadows in Newfoundland, she headed once more into the ice pack.

But this was the calm before the storm. On board was Ragnar Thorseth's 12-year-old son, also named Erik, who would not only complete the epic journey but like the rest of the crew, live to tell the tale.

For ahead, a near-hurricane was blowing up. With winds gusting 67 miles an hour (25 to 30 metres a second) and massive waves threatening to engulf the ship, Thorseth tied his 12-year-old son to a short rope attached to his waist.

Incidentally, Thorseth was criticised severely by the Norwegian popular press for taking his son, Erik, with him on the voyage. It was argued that he was missing out on his education.

Having successfully circumnavigated the globe with Saga *Siglar,* Thorseth argued that Erik had received a better education than any school child in Norway. Erik subsequently became a ship's captain.

Back in the north Atlantic, the crew of Saga *Siglar* battled the near hurricane for 15 hours and when the wind finally abated to a rather pleasant gale force, the crew counted themselves lucky that they had survived.

Indeed, Trygve Berg, who tied himself to the mast in order to film the ship in high seas, confided that he really through they would all perish.

Not long afterwards, the crew sighted icebergs off the Labrador coast and no doubt with great relief sailed into a fjord, the banks of which were lined with forests of pine.

This was the very timber so sought after by Erik the Red, Leif Eriksson and others. With timber almost non-existent in Greenland, searching for it became imperative and was one of the reasons for the Viking expansion west of Greenland.

Saga *Siglar* was the first Viking *knarr* to visit L'Anse aux Meadows in Newfoundland for a thousand years and her crew were greeted with bands, dignitaries and just about the entire population. But that, is not quite the end of the story.

Saga *Siglar* continued her voyage, sailing south down the North American coast to Boston, New York, Washington, Virginia and Florida, for all we know, still following in the wake of Leif Eriksson.

After that, she rounded the Horn to become the first Viking *knarr*, indeed the only Viking *knarr* so far as we know, ever to circumnavigate the globe. Her voyage was so successful, that Ragnar Thorseth commissioned two more Viking ships to be built.

These were replicas of the Gokstad and Oseberg ships and to mark the United Nations Childrens' Year in 1992, Saga *Siglar* again crossed the Atlantic, this time accompanied by the Gokstad replica, which had been named *Gaia,* which means *Earth Mother.*

Not long after their return, the three Viking ships once again headed for the ocean. This time, they were bound for the Mediterranean, waters in which once again a Viking ship had not been seen for ten centuries.

But as they were sailing into Valencia, disaster struck. An unexpected storm, a full Force 12 hurricane, blew up and completely overwhelmed both the new Oseberg ship and Saga *Siglar*.

Fortunately, all hands were rescued, but only after ten hours in the water and using a camera flash to attract attention.

Ragnar Thorseth, however, was not the kind of man to be beaten. He salvaged what remained of the two ships and had the wreckage transported back to Norway.

There, he and his helpers painstakingly rebuilt Saga *Siglar,* piece by piece and with 60 per cent of the ship re-assembled, she looked for all the world like the remains of the original Skuldelev *knarr* at the Viking ship museum at Roskilde in Denmark.

The Vikings captured the imagination of generations and much of what they gave to society lives on in the jewellery of the age, which a thousand years later is still made in Norway and worn around the world.

The Viking spirit lives on in the craftsmanship that they bequeathed. The exquisite Viking designs that once adorned the prow of the Oseberg ship and others like her remain popular to this day and you can see them in Norwegian craft fairs and homes throughout the land.

Above all, the spirit of the Vikings lives on in the boatbuilding techniques of men like Sigurd Bjorkedal and his sons.

They subsequently completed a second replica of the Skuldelev *knarr*, a ship identical to Saga *Siglar*.

Her name is *Kvitserk* and it means 'White dress of a Lady', a name borrowed from a glacier in Greenland.

It is through her and other ships like her, and through the men who build and sail them, that the spirit of the Vikings will, I am sure, live on for many, many more years to come.

***

Summer with Selik
A true story from Norway's west coast

The location: Teistklubben on the west coast of Norway

Some years ago, I was very privileged to be asked to produce and write the script for a television series about a young Norwegian girl who became a surrogate mother to a seal pup.

In many ways, it was the most difficult assignment that I had ever undertaken.

The principal reason for that, was that in my mind, I had to become a 17-year-old Norwegian girl.

In order to write a script in the first person – which I felt was the best way to do it – I had to think like a girl of that age.

I had to be able to speak as if I were a teenage Norwegian girl speaking English and I had to use the same kind of language that a girl of that age and nationality would use, rather than what I might write naturally.

Otherwise, the entire film would lack that element of authenticity that is so crucial when you are making a film about reality.

Aside from that, there are two very different ways of writing in the English language. The first way is to write for the eye, when you are reading and the second is for the ear, when you are listening.

If I am writing a lecture, for example, I write for the ear. To do that I have to read aloud every single word repeatedly because it is so different from written English.

The film was also very difficult to make because we decided to film everything exactly as it happened, with no script. Not even a rough shooting script. That way, we could be sure that the film would be completely genuine.

The downside of that decision was that it meant shooting video at a ratio of nearly 60 to one. In other words, we shot about 90 hours of video, roughly one hour for each minute of the programme.

Not surprisingly, when we had finished filming, it

took several weeks to view it all and to log not only each sequence, but each individual shot. I well remember the tortuous process of trying to decide which clips to use because they were all so beautifully filmed and directed by my great friend and camera operator, Trygve Berge.

I also remember trying to sort through hundreds of tiny slips of paper denoting the different scenes, and trying to place them in an order that would make sense. That said, the story itself was extremely simple with a beginning, a middle and an end, perhaps unusually these days, in that order.

Picture if you will, an early summer's day off the west Norwegian coast. The sun is shining. The sea is mirror calm and the offshore skerries are teeming with seals, mostly Harbour seals.

Nature being, as we say, red in tooth and claw, each year male killer whales or orcas, if you prefer, attack and kill a few of the mothers for reasons we do not yet understand.

Trygve Berge was well aware of this and reasoned that if his daughter, Katrine, who was just 17, searched and happened to find an abandoned seal, and then reared it until adulthood, we would have the makings of a very good and unusual television series suitable for all ages.

So, this is the story of how we made that film, which I am delighted to say was shown in 68 countries worldwide and won a variety of international awards.

The location was the small island of Teistklubben, the summer home of a local policemen who happened to be a good friend and neighbour of Trygve. As Trygve was always behind the camera, he obviously couldn't play his natural role as Katrine's father.

Instead, we called upon the policeman, Malvin Frisnes, who had never acted in his life. (No union problems in Norway!) Only six of us were involved in

making the film, which cost about £80,000. (The stills photographer at the extreme right of the top row should not have been in the production crew picture).

Sadly, Katrine's English, although good at the time, was not quite fluent enough for the commentary. So, we had to find another Norwegian girl of approximately the same age whose voice would match that of Katrine.

As she read the opening words of the script, you could hardly tell the difference!

"I love this place. The ocean. The sea air. The wind blowing through my hair. I love the smell of the seaweed and the sound of the waves, and of the wildlife, too!"

Eventually, after scouring the inner skerries, Katrine and Malvin found a lone seal pup, but we couldn't just take it there and then. We needed to wait a couple of days to make sure that its parents were not still around.

Back at Teistklubben, Katrine was so excited she could hardly eat or sleep. At this stage, she had absolutely no idea what she was letting herself in for. Nor, for that matter, did we! Hardly an hour went past without her peering through the window or gazing out to sea through her binoculars.

Two days later, the pup was still there with no sign of its parents. When Katrine stepped ashore, the pup didn't stir. It was obviously very weak from a lack of food.

"He was only two or three days old. I called him 'he' because he looked like a little boy", Katrine says in the film.

Bringing the pup back to the island was the beginning of long journey into the unknown. We had decided from the outset that we would not re-enact anything which involved the seal.

Sometimes, that meant missing good shots, but over the next three months there would be many, many others.

The journey began with a two-hour car and ferry trip to the Seaquarium at Ålesund. The seal didn't seem to mind at all – though the ferry passengers thought it all very strange indeed. Most of them had probably never seen a seal that close before.

"I think that was when I first knew I had to keep him", Katrine says, "and I had to persuade the vet to let me take him back to Teistklubben."

The vet quickly established that the little seal was in reasonably good health and that with care would certainly survive but he warned that it would not be easy.

To begin with, Katrine would have to feed the pup every four hours, day and night. She would have to teach him how to eat and how to catch fish for himself. No easy task. But she was adamant that she could handle it.

"I suppose that I had already become a kind of mother to him. That's when I decided to give him a name. I thought of Selius. And Baltus. But finally, I decided on Selik.", she adds.

The next step was to weigh him. It was important that we keep a record of his weight so that we could see that he was making progress, especially as he would have to be fed by tube for the first few weeks.

Weighing Selik was often an hilarious affair, not least because Selik was never renowned for keeping still. We first recorded ten kilos, subtracted one-and-a-half for the bucket. Eight-and-a-half kilos or nearly 19 pounds.

The vet said that in three months he would weigh about 45 kilos (100 pounds or about seven stone).

To begin with, Selik could only take liquid food, chunks of herring blended with sea water. Katrine had to learn how to force a rubber tube down his throat and squeeze the gruel down it with a plastic syringe.

The seal's throat is designed to swallow whole fish, so there was no real discomfort for him. He just sat back and enjoyed having his stomach filled with food.

The vet knew that the seal would form a bond with

 whoever fed it regularly and it was obvious that Katrine should fill that role. Too many people fussing around it would probably

confuse him.

The danger was that Katrine would become too close to the seal and treat him as a pet rather than as a wild animal. That, of course, would make it much more difficult for her when the time came to return Selik to the ocean.

We had, of course, saved the seal's life. Had we not found him and taken him to the Seaquarium, he would certainly have died from starvation within a couple of days.

Our over-riding fear, though, was entirely selfish; that something might happen to him or that he might become ill and die, leaving us with an uncompleted film having spent tens of thousands of pounds of other people's money.

The other ever-present thought in our minds was how the experience would affect Katrine. She was, after all, only 17 years old and like all teenagers very impressionable.

We were sure that there would be floods of tears when the moment came three months' hence for her to re-introduce Selik to his natural environment.

That was an element of the film for which we were well prepared but there was also the question of whether the experience would have any lasting effects or unforeseen circumstances.

For instance, if Katrine was to prepare Selik for a life at sea, she would have to learn to dive and to swim with him with the obvious potential dangers that diving might involve when swimming eight miles or so out to sea.

There was also the nagging thought that Selik might not survive when she did return him to the ocean. Would he be able to fend for himself?

For all of us, and especially for Katrine, life was suddenly full of imponderables, not least whether Trygve's vision for the film would actually materialise.

If Selik simply settled down to a routine of eating and sleeping, it would clearly be rather boring and almost impossible to sustain three 25-minute television programmes that we had promised to deliver to the Norwegian State Broadcasting Company, NRK.

The fact was that none of us had the remotest idea of what was in store. All we could do was to knuckle down to three months' of being constantly on duty.

There would be few if any breaks because we could not afford to miss anything that Selik did. There were many excellent shots that we missed simply because the camera took several seconds to warm up or because Trygve was in another room when Selik did something interesting. Happily, it all worked out extremely well in the end but there were many anxious moments.

My job didn't really start in earnest until after the film had been shot and Selik had grown to a 100-pound monster and been released.

Still at the end of each day, I would spend endless hours viewing and logging each frame of the video that Trygve had shot.

Needless to say, I ended up with a monumental file that was so big it that it was extremely difficult to find specific shots, despite a very methodical filing system.

From my point of view, it was also very important to absorb the general atmosphere of the Norwegian coastal environment and to take extensive descriptive notes of what I saw and heard. In other words, I had to

immerse myself totally into both the environment and Katrine's mind.

Nor was life particularly easy at Teistklubben.

This was Malvin's summer home. There was no electricity. We used oil lamps. We drew our water from a deep well and had to collect wood each day if we wanted a fire.

We had to do all our own cooking. There 2were no elaborate catering trucks for us with hot, three-course meals and constant mugs of coffee, as on most film sets. Nor did we have any portable toilets. Our sanitation consisted of chemical toilets, which naturally had to be emptied from time to time.

For Katrine, it was particularly hard because if she wanted a bath or to wash her hair, she had to ask Trygve to go ashore and to drive her several miles to a friend's house where there was hot water.

So, with Selik requiring food every four hours and Trygve reluctant to miss anything that happened, understanding and patience were required by all.

There was one occasion when Katrine was so tired and felt so dirty, and missed her friends so much, that she almost gave up.

Nonetheless, no matter how low she felt, her growing love for Selik always seemed to make life more tolerable. At first, Selik seemed to sleep all the time, clearly exhausted from all the travelling and because everything was so new to him.

"I did worry about him," Katrine said. "He seemed so ... defenceless! I wondered how we would be able to teach him to eat for himself and I wasn't sure how much attention I should give him, whether it was all right to pick him up so much. There were so many questions and no answers". And Selik certainly had his moments!

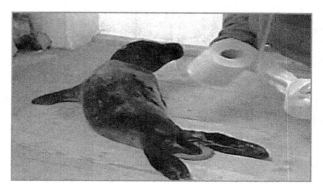

Malvin was not pleased. The seal's toiletry disasters happened once too often. From now on, he said, Selik would have to stay outside in a cage.

Fortunately, Malvin was an expert handyman and was able quickly to build a special cot. Now, Selik could sleep in the boathouse, which was probably better for him than being cooped up indoors all the time.

Malvin weaved a rope bottom to the cot so that if

Selik did make a mess, he wouldn't have to lie in it. We were learning all the time.

During the first week, we suspected that the little seal wasn't very well. In fact, Selik lost nearly two kilos – about three-and-a-half pounds, which had us all extremely worried.

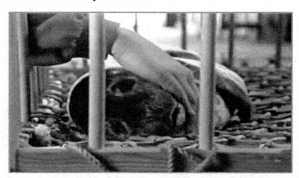

Katrine tried to jolly him along by taking him out to the skerries and introducing him to some other forms of wildlife.

Selik, however, did not seem that impressed! Still it seemed to have done him some good. Back at Teistklubben, he had definitely found his appetite again and our concerns about spending vast amounts of money for a non-film quickly evaporated, especially when Trygve captured a shot of him climbing the front door steps and hopping into the kitchen for his meal.

Suddenly, he began to gain weight and grow stronger. He also developed a very independent spirit. Measuring him was almost impossible! He just would not keep still.

"When we recorded a length of 23 inches and 30 inches on the same day, we decided to give up.," Katrine said despairingly.

As Teistklubben is fairly close to the Arctic Circle, the sun doesn't go down until nearly midnight, so the days were long and, as the Vet had predicted, it was gruelling work.

"Selik demanded so much attention and after the first week I was quite exhausted." Katrine recalled, "but he was such a joy. I'd have done anything for him then. I didn't mind how much I had to do. The only thing that really mattered was his survival and I knew only too well there would be problems enough trying to guarantee that!"

Selik was always hungry and he always let you know when he wanted his mashed herring gruel with a bark not unlike that of a fox. It was a quite demanding bark, too!

When Katrine put the tube down his throat, he would look as if we had just given him a cigar. Within a minute, a syringe full of gruel had disappeared and Selik would hop off, replete and happy.

And so, the filming continued. When Katrine took Selik down to the small lagoon just behind the house, he at first refused to be coaxed into the water.

It was as if he was frightened of it and instead of swimming off joyfully as we had anticipated, he snuggled up to Katrine's legs and then hopped ashore at the earliest opportunity, making his escape back to the safety of the house and garden.

I remember us joking about having found the only seal in the world that was scared of the sea. Except that it didn't seem that funny at the time. Still black humour does have its uses and Katrine persevered.

She talked to him all the time, almost as if he was a human, telling him that one day the ocean would be his home.

Little by little, it was almost as if Selik was listening and understood because soon, he was thoroughly enjoying his daily swim. Mind you, at that time, he was still so small that he was not strong enough to swim against the current and was constantly swept away.

But he was learning and growing stronger with the effort. There was no question, though, that he was always a lot happier on land, dozing under a bush or chasing butterflies and daisies, which was one of his favourite past-times.

By the time he was three weeks old, Selik had graduated to swallowing one-inch chunks of solid fish. He couldn't eat them himself, of course. He didn't know how to catch them. That was something we would have to teach him later. In the meantime, either the vet or Katrine had to poke the chunks down his throat with their fingers.

Selik was still eating every four to six hours, constantly demanding attention. We were getting tired, too, the long hours taking their toll. We were working from about seven o'clock in the morning until eleven o'clock at night every single day with only very short breaks for our meals.

But there were lots of good times. As the sun was going down, we would take a bottle of whisky and another of brandy, place them on the engine cowling of one of the boats and chug off to the outer skerries eight miles off shore.

Once there, we would raise a glass (or two) of whisky to the sun as it disappeared flaming beneath the horizon and toast its re-appearance shortly afterwards with a glass (or two) of brandy. Just to encourage the elements to provide us with good filming weather, the toasts arguably became a good deal more numerous than perhaps they should have done!

I seem to recall Trygve filming one or two sunsets that later proved to be out of focus! In the event, this was immaterial because Trygve became almost addicted to filming the summer sunsets and filmed so many that we lost count of them, and all exquisitely filmed.

Dawn, in this part of the world, of course, being only a couple of hours after sunset. More than once we were temporarily lost in the sea fog and only arrived back in time for coffee and some breakfast before starting yet another day.

And what wonderful days they were! It was certainly one of the happiest times of my life.

Eventually, though, the time came for Katrine to go diving with Selik. This was a time fraught with worry. Not so much for Katrine, I have to say, but because we were terrified that Selik might simply swim off and disappear, leaving us having shot only one of the three projected programmes.

On the other hand, we couldn't let Selik become too dependent on humans. We had to re-introduce him to his own environment and the sooner the better, really.

In the meantime, Katrine had completed a diving course, tutored especially by our superb underwater cameraman, Svein Halkjellsvik, a wonderful friend and colleague sadly no longer with us.

At first, Selik was clearly not enamoured by the thought of swimming in the ocean and he had a mind of his own and when he didn't want to do something. It called for the firm hand of persuasion.

To begin with, he was extremely nervous, but only for a minute or two. Then, he suddenly decided that he rather liked it and he was off exploring, cork-screwing through the swaying seaweed.

"Within a few minutes, Selik was completely at home underwater, although he never strayed very far away. He would always swim back to me," Katrine said, "usually when he needed to surface for air. Sometimes, he was as funny underwater as he was on land. He just loved to chase his tail."

At five weeks, Selik had developed an appetite like a horse. He would eat as many as ten whole fish a day, which meant that Malvin and Katrine had to go fishing every day.

Selik, of course, was not interested in whole fish at that time. He wanted them chopped up into easily digestible chunks.

Eventually, the vet suggested giving Selik bigger and bigger chunks. He would eat as much as he was given and still come back for more. Then, almost without realising it, he ate his first whole fish! Finally, we were making progress.

The challenge now would be to teach him how to *catch* a fish and how to swallow it on his own. At this juncture, we had no idea as to how we might accomplish that!

"That summer with Selik has so many memories for me now. It was idyllic", Katrine recalls. "Selik and I were as close as any two living beings could be.

"Yet almost every day, I had to tell myself that I mustn't treat him as a pet. That he was wild. "It was so difficult because in a way, he *was* a pet! He could be so endearing – and funny, too!

"These were moments that made all the hard work worth while. Just watching him trying to eat the flowers gave us endless hours of amusement.

"He didn't want to miss anything and there were times when he was a real pain, especially when he chased the lawnmower. Malvin was pretty understanding, really.

"Selik would play until he was exhausted and then just flop down and fall asleep, wherever he happened to be!"

Eventually, Trygve and the vet hit on the idea of borrowing a large tank from a local salmon farm, placing Selik in it with live fish to see if his genetic instinct would kick in and whether he would try to catch

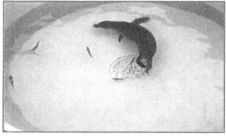

them.

He did! The only problem was that he tried to catch them all at once! He soon realised, however, that if he was to catch a fish, he would have to single it out.

Even when he had learned to do that, he still didn't know what to do with the fish, how to swallow one on his own. It was a long, long learning process for us all.

In the meantime, Selik was growing stronger and heavier all the time. Swimming in the stream at the bottom of the garden was one of his favourite pastimes.

The current was strong there and he would battle against it as if his life depended on it. In a way, it did because soon he would have to cope with even stronger currents and waves in the sea.

So, we decided to test Selik in a choppy sea and took him to the outer skerries eight miles off shore. It was an experiment that almost brought the film to a complete halt.

The sea here was much rougher than I thought and soon Selik seemed to be in real trouble. For almost an hour, the waves battered him as Katrine looked on helplessly.

Eventually, Katrine managed to grab hold of him, but it was a close call. Had Selik been dashed onto the rocks, he might easily have been knocked unconscious and drowned.

Happily, the unscheduled and potentially near fatal drama actually turned out to be a rather good ending to the second of the three programmes.

When Selik was two and a half months old, he weighed almost 32 kilos (70lbs). In the wild, he would have been almost ready to leave his mother or she him.

But although he could now catch a fish, he still hadn't learned how to eat what he caught. There was nothing really that we could do except wait and hope because the reality was that if he couldn't figure it out, we couldn't put him back into the ocean.

If we couldn't do that, we would have a film without an ending and as we couldn't look after him forever, we would probably have had to slaughter him. It was a very grim thought after all that we had been through with him!

In fact, our fears were all for nothing. One day, when he was swimming in tight circles round the tank, Selik snagged a fish and then suddenly, instead of letting it go, he flipped it up and swallowed it head first. It was most definitely a 'major key' moment for the composer of our theme music, Dave Hewson.

It was still not quite time to release Selik to the wild. We needed to be absolutely sure that he could catch and eat fish in more realistic circumstances than the salmon-farm tank.

Selik, in the meantime, was growing fast. He was much heavier. He was difficult to pick up and hold for any length of time and he was much more independent and adventurous.

Now, it was much more difficult to contain him and we were all very concerned that he would escape and head out to sea, where it is doubtful that he would have survived.

To stop him hopping away, we decided to keep him in the cot that Malvin had made for him when he was little. Selik was not amused.

"He made such a fuss that in the end I had to let him out again," Katrine remembers. "I tried to watch him but occasionally I had no alternative but to leave him for a few minutes and as events turned out that nearly cost him his life.

"Unfortunately. Selik had fallen off the wall. He was obviously concussed and in shock, so we called the vet immediately. Selik just lay there for hours, hardly moving, blood seeping from his nose. I was awful and I was in tears.

"We all thought that we were going to lose him. Even the vet seemed to be uncertain about what to do because it looked as if there was some kind of internal injury".

Eventually the vet suggested putting him back in the tank, where he would weigh less and perhaps feel more comfortable. Selik remained listless for a very long time, well over an hour, and then he began to swim a little and even made a half-hearted attempt at catching a fish.

At least putting him in the water seemed to have stopped his nose bleeding, but it would be several hours more before he showed any further signs of recovering.

"I remember wondering as he lay there whether seals have feelings and can remember things," Katrine said.

"The vet said that he would always seek human company and that every so often he would come back to harbour, or a yacht, looking for people

"That evening, Selik seemed a little better, so I carried him down to the bridge to watch the sun go down. I don't know why really. I just wanted to be alone with him, to let him know that I cared.

"My Dad had lit the fire and maybe the warmth helped because gradually Selik seemed to perk up a little and to take an interest in his surroundings again".

The next morning, life went back to normal. Selik was eating like a horse again and obviously much better, although his literary skills certainly left much to be desired.

At two-and-a-half months, Selik weighed nearly 100 pounds (45 kilos) and he was too heavy for Katrine to carry.

What's more, he was now getting decidedly grumpy. It was finally time to prepare him for the ocean.

Malvin placed nets across a small channel so that he couldn't swim out to sea and we fed him live fish. Only when we were sure he could catch and eat them would he be ready.

Frankly, we couldn't wait. Everyone was exhausted with the long hours and Selik was very hard work. Eventually, the day of release arrived. Malvin raised the net and Selik swam very slowly towards the open sea. Katrine was extremely sad, as we had anticipated.

"I tried to tell myself that this was a happy occasion – that I shouldn't be sad," she said later. "After all, we had saved Selik's life. And now look at him, as fat as any other seal in the ocean. He really did not want to go".

"It was as if he knew that once he had swum off, he would never see us again. Not until Malvin gave him a gentle nudge with his boot did he finally swim off.

"And then, he was gone. Back to the sea.

"I knew then that Teistklubben would never be quite the same again, that whenever I came back, I would always be looking out to sea, hoping for a glimpse of him and in my heart, I knew too that Selik would never be very far away, that he'd be somewhere out there, amongst the skerries".

We made *Summer with Selik* in 1992 and I think it was one of those landmark moments in all our lives.

Katrine (her real name is spelt thus, but in the film, she was 'Katrina') is now happily married to an architect and has two children. She has a masters degree in economics and is a bio-engineer, but has chosen instead to run a Yoga Centre in Bodø in northern Norway.

Svein sadly died from cancer in 2004, on his 55th birthday, much too soon.

Malvin has retired and divides his time between Spain, Norway and England visiting his daughter and grandchild.

Trygve continues to work as a cameraman but now with an eye on retirement.

In the meantime, I no longer write film scripts – just talks which enable me every so often to go to sea as a guest speaker on cruise ships.

And every time, I take a cruise to Norway, I always look out for Teistklubben and think of Selik, and that wonderful summer we all shared together.

***

OSLO

The bonus of Oslo is that your ship will berth at one of two cruise ship quays within minutes of the city centre, so shuttle buses are not necessary.

From the ship, you will be able to gaze across  the harbour, dominated by the austere twin-towered City Hall, just a five-minute walk away if you are at the nearest dock to the city. Immediately above the berth is *Akershus Fortress,* built between 1299 and the early 1300s under the rule of Håkon the Fifth.

The castle withstood several sieges and was modernised by King Christian IV, who ruled from 1577 until 1648.

Christian was a modest chap who, after a fire in the old town, built a new city closer to the fortress in 1638 and named it Christiana after himself. Later, he converted the castle into a royal residence. (The name

Christiana was abandoned in 1925 when the city was renamed Oslo).

Today, the fortress gardens are an important venue for concerts, various ceremonies and other major events, and guided tours are operated throughout the summer.

One unmissable attraction is the *Norwegian Resistance Centre* in the castle grounds. It stands in a 17th century building next to the memorial for Norwegian patriots who were executed on the same spot by German troops during the Second World War.

Although small and quite cramped, it is easy to become completed absorbed by this fascinating museum. It has a generous display of photographs, original documents, old newspapers and recordings, models, wireless sets and other wartime paraphernalia that tell the story of the five years of German occupation.

It is a bit of a climb to reach the fortress, but for those passengers with limited walking ability, there is a small shopping mall on the quayside, no more than 30 yards from the ship.

Here you can buy all the souvenirs you could possibly find elsewhere, from hand-knitted sweaters, socks, baseball caps and T-shirts bearing the Norwegian flag and other logos to a plethora of miniature trolls, replica Viking jewellery and Viking helmets with horns, which the Vikings never actually wore.

As some journalists working for the more sensational newspapers say: 'Never let facts get in the

 way of a good story'.

Some of the shops here even sell boxer shorts designed with copulating reindeer, an indicator perhaps of the Norwegians' sense of humour.

Just a five-minute walk from the berths is the *City Hall* or *Rådhus* (pronounced *roared, as in cord, hoose*). This is the administrative centre and home of the City Council.

If you are fortunate enough to visit Oslo on the first Wednesday of the month, you may hear a carillon concert ringing out over the vast square and harbour that front the building. You can pre-book tours of the City Hall year-round by telephone or email, the address of which is: *postmottak@rft.oslo.kommune.no* and the phone number is (+47) 23 46 12 00.

The tours, for up to 30 people, are well worth the effort of pre-booking as many of the rooms are decorated with huge murals from the first half of the 20th century, depicting Norwegian history, culture and working life, especially fishing.

The Central Hall is where the annual Nobel Peace Prize awards are presented, usually by the King.

Opposite to the ship's birth, on the other side of the

harbour, is a restaurant and shopping area, a delightful spot to sit with a coffee or a beer overlooking the harbour.

You will, of course, need a

mortgage to buy either, much less a meal. A lager is likely to cost you as much as £8-10 ($13-$15 or €11-13) in Norway, which in 2011 was ranked as the second most expensive city in the world for living expenses after Tokyo.

Since then, it has dropped back to ninth, but Norway is still hugely expensive. A small pizza and a medium-small glass of wine for two is likely to knock you back around £60, which, at the time of writing, is around $77 or €67.

That said, Oswegians, as they are known, have an enviable quality of living as do all Norwegians, which helps to make up for the expenses.

Geographically, Oslo is one of the world's largest capitals despite a fairly meagre population of 672,061 in the municipality and a little more than a million in the urban area.

This rapid growth is mostly due to high birth rates and immigration. Today, the immigrant population is growing more quickly than the Norwegian and if you include people born in Oslo of immigrant parents, they currently represent more than a quarter of the city's total population.

Nonetheless, with greater Oslo covering an area of 175 square miles, the city is, in fact, the least densely populated capital city in Europe.

Across the harbour, opposite to Akershus Fortress, is *Akersbrygge,* boardwalk lined with restaurants and bars behind which lies an attractive shopping area with all the main design and fashion chains, more restaurants and wide pedestrian boulevards sectioned by canals and bridges.

Akersbrygge runs into an area called *Tjuvholmen (Thief's headland),* mostly built on reclaimed land. Here, intriguing architecture and modernistic buildings are home to offices, apartments, galleries and art installations, not least the *Astrup Fearnley Museum* at Strandpromenaden No.2.

This architectural gem designed by Renzo Piano holds the largest collection of modern art in Norway and also boasts a sculpture park and a small beach.

Opened in 1993, the museum is owned privately, funded by the descendants of one of Norway's leading shipping families.

It specialises in international contemporary art, much of it from America, the most spectacular piece being Jeff Koon's huge sculpture of the pop star, Michael Jackson, with his favourite chimpanzee, Bubbles – a piece of art that set the museum back more than five million dollars. Britain's Damien Hirst also has several works there.

The museum holds at least half a dozen temporary exhibitions each year in addition to its permanent collection comprising Norwegian and international art.

Opening times are Tuesday-Wednesday and Thursday from 12 noon-5pm, Thursday 12 noon-7pm and weekends 11am-5pm. Mondays closed.

The entrance fee is NOK 130 £11.70, $14.45, €13.10).

In a bay behind Akershus Fortress and the ship's berth (turn right from the ship and walk round the headland) is *Oslo's Opera House*, gleaming white and notable for its sloping, angular 'z'-shaped design that invites you to walk along its roof. With a forecourt dipping gently down to the water's edge, it is a fabulous place to experience panoramic views of the city, the fjord and its islands year-round.

At first sight, Oslo may seem a little parochial, a cosy little town where everything is close to the ship. You would be right – but, you could easily spend a week in this city and not see everything.

Happily, almost all the main attractions are reasonably close to the city centre.

Just a short and most enjoyable ferry ride from the harbour takes you to the Bygdøy peninsula.

This is the home of *The Fram Museum, The Kon Tiki Museum, The Norwegian Maritime Museum, The Viking Ship Museum, and the Norwegian Museum of Cultural History.*

The Bygdøy ferry operates from the harbour between March and October, departing every 20-30 minutes.

Bygdøy is one of the most popular attractions in Oslo and you could comfortably spend an entire day here, if not two days. You can buy combination tickets for the first three of the museums listed above!

The Fram Museum is home to the three-masted polar ship *Fram,* which was used by all Norway's renowned explorers – Fritjiof Nansen, Otto Sverdrup, Roald Amundsen and others.

Fram is said to be the strongest wooden ship ever built, having survived the harshest weather and ice conditions in both the Arctic and Antarctic, and having sailed further north and south than any other wooden ship.

The exhibition not only demonstrates how the crew and their husky teams survived these conditions in reasonable comfort over extended periods but also boasts a simulator in which you can feel the cold and dangers facing polar explorers more than a century ago.

Adjacent to the museum, is the smaller *Gjoa Museum* which covers the Arctic and Northwest Passage.

Gjoa was the sloop which Roald Amundsen chose to sail through the entire length of the Northwest passage in 1903, the first person to do so.

It would be another 76 years before that feat was accomplished again, by Ragnar Thorseth and Trygve Berge in 1979.

The *Kon-Tiki Museum* is devoted to the exploits of Tor Heyerdahl, who ranks as one of Norway's most famous explorers.

Heyerdahl came to the world's attention in 1947 when he built *Kon-Tiki,* a pre-Columbian style raft made with balsa wood which he sailed across the Pacific from Peru to Polynesia.

The adventurer was trying to prove that people from the west coast of South America discovered, or at least sailed to, Easter Island, a contention that experts subsequently dismissed.

Nevertheless, Heyerdahl conducted important experiments as to how the first settlers on Easter Island might have moved the mysterious stone statues for which the island is famous. He also carried out significant excavations on Easter Island as well as in the pre-historic site in Túcume, Peru.

Two years after the voyage, Heyerdahl's film of the Kon-Tiki expedition won an Academy Award for Best Documentary, which you can watch in the museum.

Heyerdahl, was one of the earliest champions of the environment and its protection using *Ra II,* a boat made from reeds to publicise his involvement during a voyage from North Africa to the Caribbean.

The *Kon-tiki* and *Ra* vessels are both on display, as are maps, documents, photographs and film – as well as a library comprising several thousand books.

The museum is open year-round from 10 am, closing between 4pm and 6pm depending on the time of year. Entry tickets vary from £5 ($6.50, €5.60) for students to £12 ($15.40, €13.46) for adults with concessions for seniors.

Perhaps the most famous of this clutch of museums is **The Viking Ship Museum**, which houses the world's best-preserved Viking ships and artefacts discovered along the Oslo fjord.

The best-known ships are the Oseberg ship with its extraordinary ornate prow. Discovered in 1903, she was used as a ceremonial ship.

The Oseberg grave also contained two Viking women, a large number of textiles, exquisitely carved animal heads, a cart and a sleigh.

Also on display is the Goskad ship, a fast ocean-going ship used for Viking raids. A Viking male buried in it had severe cuts to his legs, a sure indication that he died fighting.

The museum offers a unique visual tour of the Viking age through a film which depicts the building, sailing and burial of a Viking ship, all projected onto the museum ceiling.

For anyone interested in the Vikings, their ships and artefacts, this is a 'must-see' museum.

Nearby are the **Norwegian Maritime Museum** and the **Museum of Cultural History.** The former offers a variety of exhibitions throughout the year and offers trips on some of the vessels it displays outdoors.

The latter offers a unique look at Norwegian folk and church art, paintings, costumes, weapons and the lifestyles of Norwegians, including the Sami culture and traditions, from the 16th century to the 1900s.

The open-air museum is also said to be Europe's largest, comprising more than 150 homes and other buildings from different parts of the country.

In many of these there are separate exhibitions and displays giving a unique insight into how Norwegians lived in both town and country through the ages.

For ship's passengers who prefer to escape from the hurly-burly of city life and into the country, this is an ideal choice.

Another benefit of Oslo is that it is just as interesting and perhaps even more fun and atmospheric in winter, when some cruise ships visit on Christmas cruises to the Scandinavian capitals.

Christmastime in the main shopping area

The heart of Oslo is just a short walk from the ship's berth.

If you walk towards the City Hall, cross the main road and walk up and to the end of Rosenkrantzgate or Nedre Vollgate (the 3rd and 4th roads to the right of the City Hall) you will arrive outside the parliament building (to your right).

Christmastime in the main shopping area, the Norwegian Parliament and next to it on the left, the Grand Hotel

The Grand Hotel lies on Karl Johans Gate, which is the main thoroughfare leading to the Royal Palace to the left and, to the right, to the main shopping area, cathedral, railway station and the Tourist Information Office, the entrance to which is tucked away to the left of the railway station.

The Grand Hotel café, incidentally, is full of atmosphere and a great place to have a light lunch.

Karl Johans Gate and the Royal Palace

Directly opposite to the parliament building and running adjacent to Karl Johans Gate all the way to the National Gallery and Royal Palace is a narrow park.

Here, in summer, there are several outdoor restaurants and, in winter, an outdoor ice-skating rink.

If Norwegian children are said to be born on skis, they are no strangers to ice skates, either, and you can spend an enjoyable half hour watching them learning to skate here.

Ice skating in the centre of Oslo. It is often said that Norwegian children are born on skis!

If by then you are beginning to feel the chill of Oslo in winter, what better than to retire to one of the many atmospheric restaurants, where, if you are as hardy as the Norwegians, you can eat outdoors? Indoors, however, is much more crowded – and fun!

Slightly further afield are the *Munch museum, Vigeland's Park* in Frogner and the *Holmenkollen* ski jump and viewpoint.

The Munch Museum houses more than half of Edvard Munch's paintings and prints. Munch, famed for his painting *The Scream*, bequeathed more than half of his paintings and prints to the museum in 1940, four years before he died.

The collection comprises nearly 1,200 paintings and some 18,000 prints as well as more than 7,000 drawings. As well as documents, art tools and other items.

The museum, which is situated at Tøyengaten 53 can be reached by the No.20 bus to Munchmuseet or on all eastbound T-Bana (metro) trains to Tøyen. The museum is accessible to disabled visitors with free admission for one companion. It is open every day from May until September from 10am until 1600 am. Entrance fees range from NOK 60 (about £5.46, $7.00, €6.12) for students and groups of more than ten people, so it pays to go as a group as the adult fee is twice that amount.

Vigeland's Park, which is actually part of Frogner Park, is an extraordinary venue comprises more than reliefs and 200 mammoth sculptures in granite, bronze and wrought iron, almost exclusively of human figures in a weird and surreal variety of poses.

Gustav Vigeland created the installation between 1924 and 1943. Among the best-known sculptures are *Angry Boy,* which depicts a naked child throwing a tantrum, *The Fountain,* which is surrounded by 20 statues representing various stages of life from birth to death, *the Monolith Plateau,* which comprises a granite monolith (a kind of totem pole) more than 14 metres (46ft) high.

Created from a single block of stone, it depicts a mass of writhing, naked humans all climbing over each other in a desperate bit to reach the top.

This is an attraction that can only be described as strange, bizarre and wonderful, and well worth a visit.

Holmenkollen Ski Jump and Museum. The museum is located beneath the famous ski jump and takes the visitor through more than 4,000 years of skiing history, including polar exploration and snowboarding.

An elevator will take you to an observation deck on top of the jump tower from which there are fabulous views of Oslo, the Oslo Fjord, and surrounding countryside.

It is, however, not for the faint hearted. Anyone who suffers even from mild acrophobia (vertigo) should think twice. For the brave, there is also a simulator of what it is like to jump.

The best way to get there is by the T-bana (Metro) which stops at the ski-jump. There is, however a steep 10-12 minute walk to the museum. Afternoons are often the best time to go to avoid queues (lines). The pay desk will advise you how long you will have to wait for the elevator to the top.

Like Vigeland's Park, Holmenkollen is open year-round and June, July and August from 9am to 8pm. Entrance fees for the jump and the museum are NOK 140 (£12.75, $16.40, €14.28) for adults and NOK 70 for 6-18 year olds. Students and seniors get in for NOK

120. It's not cheap – but the views alone make it worth it.

***

STAVANGER

Stavanger is a relatively small city for wandering, strolling and getting temporarily lost in the narrow, cobbled streets lined with white clapboard houses, sadly all too often dwarfed by monster cruise ships.

It is a city of great charm, the fourth largest in Norway, yet with a population of only a few more than 130,000 people. The majority live in the outer suburbs of Greater Stavanger, leaving the inner city with a cosy, intimate feel to it.

The Harbour, an inlet from the larger bay, evolved from a fishing port to a marina and is now the third largest cruise port in Norway. It is also one of the fastest growing cruise ports in Europe.

At least two of the largest cruise ships can moor next to the bustling market, shops, restaurants and cafes. There is no cruise terminal and most of the main sights are within a very short walk.

A small fish market lies at the head of the harbour, overlooked by a sloping market square and the 12th century Anglo-Norman *Cathedral (Domkirke) of St. Swithun,* so named after an early Bishop of Winchester.

The Cathedral was built in 1125, probably by English artisans under the direction of Bishop Reinald of Winchester. Its completion marks the accepted date on which Stavanger was founded. However, some Norwegian historians believe the town had city functions before that. There is also a possibility that an older, wooden church existed below the cathedral, so it is likely that the Cathedral was built before Stavanger was given city status.

Ravaged by fire in 1272, the *Domkirke,* was restored in the late 13th and early 14th centuries.

Sadly, it lost most of its original external and internal appearance during a renovation in the 1860s, but this was rectified between 1939 and 1964, with a further restoration in 1999.

The *Domkirke* is the only church in Norway that has been in continuous use since the 14th century.

Perhaps its most striking feature is the magnificent pulpit which dates to 1650.

Looking down from the Cathedral and marketplace, **The Old Town,** once the home of workers in the sardine canning industry, lies on the peninsula to the right of the marina and fish market.

Despite the town's ancient history, most of the wooden houses, many of which are adorned with colourful flower pots, date back to the 18th and 19th centuries.

The real joy of Stavanger is that it is mostly a pedestrian area with occasional concerts in the small squares and a vegetable market in front of the Cathedral. Here, you can buy fresh produce every day of the year directly from the local farmers.

Concert in Old Town's main square and below, the Flower and vegetable market and harbour.

Unfortunately, the market has been invaded by stallholders selling more mundane products such as T-shirts, leather belts, African wood carvings and trinketry jewellery, although it is still worth a visit.

Beyond the Cathedral, ***Breiavatnet,*** is a medium sized lake around which it is a delight to walk, pausing now and again to feed the swans and ducks, and generally relax in the sea-fresh air.

Beware, though, Norway has had a generous immigration policy, the downside of which is that there are now numerous beggars. In Stavanger, they are not particularly aggressive but almost all of them have mobile phones, which suggests that they are probably controlled by gangs.

Walking back to the Old Town, try not to miss *The Norwegian Canning Museum*, a small gem which is often overlooked. In Norwegian, it is known as the *Hermetikk Museum* and is located in what used to be a canning factory at Øvre Strandgate 88.

You might not feel that sardines, brisling and fish balls are the most exciting products to warrant a museum exhibition, but you can spend a fascinating hour or more here, learning everything you need to know from an enthusiastic staff about the canning industry, from the arrival of the fish to 'threading' them, packing and sealing them, to labelling the cans and marketing them.

Although quite small, the museum takes visitors into a world of what used to be a huge industry, with some 70 per cent of Norway's total exports of canned fish emanating from Stavanger.

In fact, more than 25 per cent of the country's canning factories were based in Stavanger until the end of the 1970s, when the herring shoals began to collapse.

By the end of the 1980s, there were less than half a dozen factories left in the entire country. After that, Norway increased its exports of salmon and other sea fish and today boasts a multi-billion kroner industry that sells fish to almost every country in the world.

It is very much a 'hands on' museum where you can try on the clothing worn by workers in the industry's heyday, try every step of the production process yourself (a huge bonus if you visit with children) and experiment by fitting fake sardines into a can. After that, if you are lucky, you may even be able to taste some sardines freshly smoked especially for you.

There is also an authentic worker's cottage from the 1800s to give an extra feel for the period.

The museum is open from May 15 to September 15 every day except Monday from 11am to 3pm (4pm at weekends). Entrance fees range from NOK 50 (£4.50, $5.85, 5.12) for students and children aged between six and 18 to NOK 95 (£8.60, $11.10, €9,75) for adults with a NOK 20 (£1.82, $2.34, €2.05) discount for seniors.

Another unlikely museum is *The **Norwegian** Petroleum Museum (Norsk Oljemuseum)*.

Who would have thought oil might be of general interest? But it is and this is a museum for visitors of all ages, explaining as it does how oil and gas are created, discovered and produced – and the products in which they are used as ingredients. It's fascinating and you will need at least an hour, if not two, to see it.

Oil was first discovered in the North Sea in the late 1960s and after various committees finally came to a decision became the principal industry in Norway with Stavanger as the main oil base.

It transformed Stavanger and brought untold wealth to Norway, ultimately ensuring the country's infrastructure and overall wealth for a century or more.

The first company to start drilling was Esso, who used a semi-submersible drilling vessel which had to be towed from New Orleans. Drilling began on the 19th July just over 100 miles southwest of Stavanger.

The oil industry was not without its dangers and disasters. In March, 1980, a semi-submersible drilling rig named after the Norwegian novelist and dramatist Alexander Lange Kielland capsized in the Ekofisk oil field about 200 miles east of Dundee in Scotland.

The rig was being used as a 'flotel' (living and recreational quarters) for men working on the production platform *Edda* nearby.

Just before 6.30 pm, the men on board heard a loud 'crack' and felt sudden heavy vibration. Within 25 minutes, the rig had listed to 30 degrees and all six anchor chains had snapped. Immediately afterwards, one of the three massive legs snapped off.

Of the 212 men on board, only 89 were saved. Most of the 123 men who lost their lives had been trapped in the cinema or the mess hall, or drowned in the heavy seas.

(At the time, a Force 8 gale was blowing and the waves were 30-35 feet high).

In order to discover the cause of the disaster, the rig had to be re-floated and towed back to Stavanger, where it took three attempts to right it.

The enormity of the project to raise it is difficult to grasp operation.

It took several months of 1983 to complete and people said it was roughly equivalent to up-ending the Albert Hall in London.

The night's work revealed the full
horror and turmoil of that night in
March 1980 when the rig toppled over
in just 30 minutes as 123 men
desperately scrambled to get out – unsuccessfully.

These pictures, turned on their side,
give an idea of the huge of the rig.

In some of the
windows you could
just see the
jumble of beds and
bunks and other
wreckage. The yellow
bags are from a previous
(puny) attempt to right
the ill-fated rig.

September 13th, 1983.

STAVANGER,
September 11,
1983

For the first time one could
see the accommodation units emerge
from the deep as the rig moved
to 45°. The reason for the project is
essentially emotional. relatives want
to recover the 35 bodies (or remains).
But many experts are interested
in the rig itself – because what they
find may be the deciding factor in
more than 20 legal actions involving £1350 mill.a

The coastguard taking a keen interest. if the
rig sinks, he gets a guaranteed blemish.

178

The collapse of the Alexander Kielland rig was the worst disaster in Norway's offshore history. An investigation later concluded that the accident was caused by metal fatigue and poor welding in one of the spars connecting the broken leg to the rest of the rig.

After missing bodies had been recovered and the investigation completed, the rig was finally scuttled in a fjord nearby.

Part of the broken spar is now on display in the Norwegian Petroleum Museum, which the Visit Norway organisation describes as comprising 'objects, models, film and interactive exhibits to illustrate everything from everyday life offshore to technology and dramatic incidents'.

An English language 3D movie is shown in the cinema throughout the day and for the children there is a 'catastrophe room and rescue chute'. There is also a café with sea views serving light meals.

The museum is open throughout the year from 10 am until 4pm. Tickets costs NOK 120 (£10.92, $14.04, €12.30) for adults with similar discounts as all museums for children, students and seniors.

Many ships run excursions to **Preikestolen (The Pulpit Rock), Lysefjord**, one of Norway's most iconic attractions, attracting about quarter of a million tourists each year.

You can either view this massive, 604 metre (1,981 ft) cliff from the 26-mile (42-metre) long fjord either from a sightseeing boat, of which there are many, or by road and hiking there.

From fjord level, the rock looks like an upended wedge topped by a plateau measuring approximately 25 x 25 metres (82 x 82 ft).

It was formed some 10,000 years ago when a glacier began to melt, releasing the pressure on the rock, which then split open. At some stage after that, huge blocks of rock adjacent to Preikestolen broke away and plunged into the fjord below.

For those who have no fear of heights and wish to stand on the plateau and admire stunning views of the entire length of Lysefjord, you can take a bus to Tau Mountain Lodge. (In 2019, a tunnel was opened to Tau making the enjoyable car ferry ride defunct).

From there, an undulating hike of about 4-5 hours and rising some 350 metres (1,150 feet) takes you to the top.

This may be tight timing if your ship is in Stavanger for a limited time, but if you do go, you should wear stout footwear, warm clothing and take food and preferably hot drinks with you.

The hike requires a high degree of fitness and it is recommended to take walking poles. Be sure also to check the time of sunset and don't set out too late or you may find yourself trapped.

For almost all passengers, the sightseeing boats are the better option.

Another extremely pleasant day out is to visit *Flor og Fjaere,* which means *Flowers and Feathers.* This is a private island garden that the owners like to describe as where the rainbow hit earth.

This is a delightful attraction, beginning with a 20-minute boat trip from Stavanger harbour and followed by wandering through the colourful gardens in which each year, the gardeners plant some 50,000 flowers.

The owner, Olav Bryn and his wife, Siri, redesign the gardens during the winter, always striving to achieve new colour and plant combinations

There is also a restaurant serving everything from creamy fish soup to Rogaland lamb, vegetarian chilli, an Indian Aloo Methi and various fish dishes. The gardens are open every day except Sundays from 4th May until 21st September with departures at 12 am and 5pm.

All visits have to be pre-booked (unless you are on an organised ship's excursion) and include the boat trip, garden tour and a restaurant meal sold as a package for NOK 1,290 (£120, $150, €132) on weekdays and NOK 1,390 (£126, $162, €142) on Sundays.

***

HAUGESUND

Lying between Stavanger and Bergen, amongst countless fjords and small islands, Haugesund is a small town with a population of just over 37,000 inhabitants, although it is the regional centre for approximately 100,000 people.

The Haugesund region is justly known as 'The Home of the Vikings', not least because it was here that Harald Fairhair became Norway's first king.

The town of *Haugesund*, meanwhile, is an unspoiled gem. A short, five-minute ride on the shuttle bus or a panoramic drive will take you from your berth on the island of Risøya across a high bridge with a commanding view of the inner channel to the town centre.

This is a tranquil place in which the principal architectural attractions are an attractive, modern church and the 75-year-old Town Hall with its prominent pink façade and corner section embellished with eight columns.

Opened in 1931, the building was a gift from a Norwegian shipowner and Liberal Party politician, Knut Knutsen (who died in 2001). The Town Hall is now one of the most well-known buildings in the country. Some people say it is the only pink Town Hall in the world.

The shopping area is both charming and modern at the same time and the main pedestrian street, appropriately named Haraldsgate, boasts plenty of individual shops and shopping malls to cater for all tastes. Indeed, it is said that there are too many shopping malls for the size of the population and that, as a result, trade is faltering.

Having explored the town, an ideal way to relax is to wander along the *Indre Kay (Inner Quay)* between Risøya bridge and, at the far end of the channel, a smaller bridge linking the town to a small island called Hasseløya.

Lined with brightly painted red, orange, yellow and white wooden buildings, the quay is a favourite summer venue for both local people and tourists, with a variety of riverside restaurants in which to taste the delicious Norwegian coastal cuisine.

What better than to sit down at one of the outdoor restaurants with a rich cream of fish soup laden with the catch of the day – shrimps, mussels and salmon with fennel, saffron and apple and just watch the world go by?

The soup was one of the best fish soups I have ever tasted and the huge pile of shrimps on toast equally so.

When you are replete and don't feel like walking too far, take a stroll to Brugata Bridge, which takes you to the tiny island of Hasseløya.

Cross the bridge and just a few yards away, to your right at the end of it, you can find a small part in which there is the small but delightful *Dokken Open Air museum.*

Here, there is a collection of old wooden boathouses, a general store, a cooperage. and a salting plant for the herring dating back to the 1860s and the heyday of the herring industry.

The main boathouse is built in Viking style with a high roof (to accommodate boat masts) and fabulously carved roof and wall supports.

There is also a photographic exhibition portraying the social lives of the people who lived here.

The entrance fee is just NOK 50 (4.50, $5.85, €5.15) and concessions for seniors and students.

Viking chieftains and kings ruled Norway for more than 500 years and Haugesund, arguably, was Norway's birthplace.

The town and most of the Haugesund region are protected from Atlantic storms by the islands of Karmøy and Røvaer, and the Karmsund strait between them enabled ships to sail to and from the town, sheltered from the open ocean.

The passage eventually became known as *Norveg* the 'North Way', from which Norway derives its name.

Harald Hårfagre, or Harald Fairhair in the anglicised version, was a powerful local chieftain who became the first king of Norway. He built his castle at ***Avaldsnes***, which lies a six mile (nine-kilometre) or 15-minute drive south of the town to the island of Karmøy.

This is also the location of the ***Nordvegen History Centre*** which could just as well have been called the ***Nordvegen Viking Heritage Centre.***

Each year, a Viking festival is held here with strolling musicians playing replica Viking instruments, Viking feasts (including roast pig), a variety of stalls demonstrating Viking tools and utensils, and local people by the score dressed up as Vikings.

You can take the No. 210 bus which runs every hour from Torggata in Haugesund costing £2 each way or a taxi for £20-£23 (NOK 220, $26, €22).

Here you can visit a reconstructed Viking farm and learn pretty much everything there is to know about Viking life in the Haugesund region, much of it from the Sagas, skaldic poems and old songs but through films, sound clips, lighting and modern technology.

The farm lies a ten-minute walk from St. Olav's Church, built by King Håkon Håkonsson around 1250 close to where an earlier king, Olav Trygvasson, is said to have drowned a group of wizards in 998.

(King Olaf brought Christianity to Norway around the year 995 and is believed to be Harald Fairhair's great grandson).

St. Olav's was a church for pilgrims, who had to enter from the north side of the church through what is now a bricked-up door. For reasons best known to themselves, pilgrims had to enter any church with their backs to the North.

On the walls of the church, you can still see runes carved or scratched nearly a thousand years ago.

The History Centre provides visitors with a glimpse of the world of magic, sorcerers, shield maidens and Norse Gods in which the Vikings believed prior to the advent of Christianity.

The farm comprises a longhouse, a boathouse for a long ship (i.e. a war ship), and several smaller buildings and is also the venue for an annual Viking Festival.

Finally, there is, of course, a souvenir shop selling books, Viking jewellery and other replica artefacts, as well as some more modern local products such as woolly hats and socks.

Harald Fairhair was buried at **Haraldshaugen,** a burial mound which is also close to the town. Here, a five-foot (1½-metre) high granite obelisk was raised in 1872 to mark the 1,000[th] anniversary of the Battle of Hafrsfjord in 872, which resulted in the unification of western Norway under a single king for the first time in the nation's history.

Back in the town, a 'must see' museum is the **Karmsund Folkemuseum (Karmsund History Museum)** on Skaaregata, next to the church. The museum gives a superb feel for the history of the town and surrounding region.

A 25-minute introductory film takes viewers by helicopter over the Haugesund region, sweeping over mountains and through gorges, which, if you are overly sensitive or suffer from motion sickness may leave you feeling a little 'air sick'.

The museum comprises several 'scenes' reproducing turn of the century sitting rooms, workshops, an old shoe shop, general store, kitchens and a school room from 1910 as well as a considerable array of artefacts, including farming tools, household utensils and artefacts from the fishing and shipping industries.

The museum's opening times vary according to the season but usually 10 am to 4 pm, although it closes at 2pm from September to February.

Ticket prices are the same as for the Dokken Open

Air Museum and you can visit both on the same ticket in summer.

If you missed the Hermetikk Canning Museum in Stavanger, you get a second chance in Haugesund at the ***H. J. Kyvik Herring Factory.***

Run by five generations of the Kyvik family since 1866, the factory is still producing '*sursild*' or pickled herring.

Consequently, the current owners are extremely knowledgeable about the salting, seasoning, preservation, refining and canning of what they describe as 'this 11-inch (28cm) fish we call 'the silver of the sea'.

You will also have the opportunity to taste the different varieties of this typical Norwegian speciality – *sild* in tomato sauce, or sour cream, mustard and in slices. The Kyviks, incidentally, are the only producers of *sursild*, a sweet-sour version of fermented herring, in Norway.

After the herring collapse, Haugesund, like Stavanger focussed instead on the oil industry to boost its economy.

Another museum well worth a visit is the ***Arquebus War History Museum***, which is located six miles (10 kilometres) or a 15-minute drive from Haugesund at the

innermost point of Førresfjord.

Covering more than 2,000 metres, this is one of Norway's largest World War II museums, covering the history of the German occupation from April, 1940 until the end of the Second World War. No stone is left unturned here – literally. There is even a reconstructed street with tanks and mountains of rubble.

The story of everyday life and of the Resistance with weapons drops, radio spies and wireless equipment, is told using vehicles and no fewer than 125 mannequins in full wartime regalia and with their equipment.

The exhibitions cover the 1940 battles in Norway, the merchant trade during the war, air strikes, German coastal artillery and, of course, the relief brought by the liberation and its aftermath. There are special exhibitions on other aspects of the war, including the defeat of Germany in Berlin in 1945.

There is a shop selling books, clothes, military knickknacks and souvenirs and also a kiosk selling coffee, tea and soft drinks.

The entrance fee of NOK 75 (£6.75, $8.75, €7.70) with the usual discounts for seniors and students represents excellent value.

A popular excursion for cruise passengers is **Åkrafjord and the Langfoss waterfall**, an hour and a half's drive through gorgeous scenery passing farms, along fjords, lakes and rugged mountains. The trip is worth it just for the views – and *Langfoss* (which means 'long fall') is described as one of the ten most beautiful waterfalls in the world.

What makes this waterfall so fascinating is the combination of its width – 205 feet (62 metres) and the fact that the water cascades down the rocks 2,007 feet (612 metres) rather than falling vertically.

The best views of the falls are from a boat on Åkrafjord, which is 20 miles (42 kms) long and has a maximum depth of 2,130 feet (650 metres) or from a farm nearby. The best time to see *Langfoss* is between June and September, when the weather is finest

Another great viewpoint, perhaps on the return journey to Haugesund, is **Mount Steinsfjellet.** To describe this 774-foot (236 metre) hump as a mountain is perhaps a little excessive, but it does offer fabulous views of Haugesund, its surroundings and the Haugesund coastline.

If you would prefer to stay on the coast, however, and have a shorter journey, **Old Skudeneshavn** on the southern tip of Karmøy island is your best bet as it is only a 45-50-minute drive from Haugesund. This beautiful, charming and 'old-worldy' little town, one of the smallest in Norway, has only 3,364 residents, who

 live in gleaming white wooden houses along narrow streets in which the smell of fresh waffles and coffee lure

you into quaint cafes.

Skudeneshavn is said to be one of the best-kept towns in the whole of Europe and if you are lucky enough to be there on Thursday to Sunday at the end of June- beginning of July, you should not miss the chance to see the 'boating festival'.

The idyllic harbour is the venue for this, the largest assembly of old wooden boats, vintage boats, tall ships and every other kind of boat you can imagine with market stalls along the quayside and oodles of atmosphere to be enjoyed.

There is a 'Time Travel' app, which you can download in order to learn about the colourful characters of the past and be guided around the town.

Protected by Norway's Cultural Heritage Act, the town is unusual because no two houses are the same. At the top of the main street is the local park with its welcoming ship's figurehead. There is even a 'moonstone' here that is believed to have been deposited by a glacier and which, some say, may be 800 million years old. Enjoy the views here, too.

Moonstone or not, Skudeneshavn is a real gem – never to be forgotten once you have been there.

***

BERGEN

Bergen is Norway's second biggest city, draped along a peninsula, surrounded by fjords and cradled by seven mountains, and that, arguably, makes it one of the most beautiful cities in Norway. When Woody Allen visited Bergen in 1988, he observed that there was "enough scenery for a dozen films", and, quite rightly, Bergen calls itself the capital of the fjord country.

It is a city of steep hillsides, old wooden houses, quiet cobbled streets, bustling markets and tranquil parks. It's a laid-back, easy-going town with a nautical air in which fish and fishing continue to underpin the local economy.

It's a booming, bustling, modern city with a wide choice of art galleries, restaurants and nightlife, and which combines its modernity with a deep reverence for its history.

Bergen is said to have been founded in 1070 AD by the Viking King, Olav Kyrre. In fact, it is probably much older. Recent archaeological finds have dated the earliest settlements there to about 50 BC or even earlier.

There is an amusing anecdote that during the city's official 900th anniversary celebrations in 1970, King Olav the Fifth visited an archaeological excavation and asked one of the city councillors: "How old is the city, really?"

To which the councillor replied: "That depends your Majesty on the amounts appropriated for further excavation."

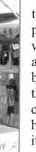

And in a way, that typifies the people of Bergen, who are known as "Bergenser", because mirth is the city's currency of life; humour among its better-known exports. They *have* to have a sense of humour because with rain sweeping in suddenly from the North Sea, Bergen is one of the wettest places in all Norway.

Indeed, local wits argue that the city emblem ought to be the umbrella. One young boy, stopped by a tourist who asked if it always rains in Bergen, allegedly replied: "I don't know. I'm only 13".

The Bergenser consider themselves almost a separate people. They are fiercely proud. Bergen is to them the least Norwegian of all Norwegian cities and they regard the rest of Norway as being, well, rather provincial.

That is not really very surprising, given that the city, right from Viking times, was always an international trading port, geographically isolated from the rest of inland Norway by the mountains.

Until the Bergen railway, eastward over the high plateau to Oslo, was opened in November 1909, Bergen was isolated from the rest of Norway except by sea and Scotland by ship was closer than the Norwegian capital; England less distant than Copenhagen.

As the westernmost city in Scandinavia, Bergen soon became a crossroads of the north. In the 13th century, Hanseatic tradesmen established a commercial community at the harbour. Full riggers plied the port with peak traffic in 1644, when more than 400 ships docked from Scotland alone.

Depending on their size, some cruise ships berth just half a mile from the city centre; others in a different fjord which entails a short shuttle bus transfer through one of several tunnels, one of them six miles long, linking the city to the rest of Norway.

If you dock close to the city centre, your first port of call may be to the Fisheries *Museum* adjacent to your berth.

This tells the story of Norwegian fishermen and how the industry has developed. It's won several prizes and become a model for similar museums around the world.

Next, if you cross the road and walk through a small gate leading to what appears to be a garden or alternatively walk 100 yards or so towards the town, you will see *Håkonshallen and the Rosenkrantz tower* on your left.

King Håkon Håkonsson built this Gothic royal residence and festival hall between 1247 and 1261 and the banqueting hall is still used by the royal family for official dinners and ceremonies.

Bergen at that time was the political hub of Norway and it was in *Håkonshallen* that officials drew up the country's first laws.

Entrance fees are NOK 100 (£9.05, $11.65, €10.25) for adults and half price for students. The museum, however, does not take credit cards – only Norwegian kroner.

Nearby is the ***Rosenkrantz Tower (The Bergen City Museum).*** The tower is named after Erik Rosenkrantz, who was the governor of Bergen castle in the 1560s, although parts of the tower were built in the 1270s.

The first great occasion celebrated within its walls was the marriage of King Magnus the Lawmender and Princess Ingeborg of Denmark, to which more than 1,000 dignitaries were invited. The party, it's said, lasted for three days and nights.

Later, the cellar was transformed into a much-feared dungeon that was in use until the late 1800s. There is a small café here offering free tea and coffee, which is included in the price of your ticket. The entrance fee is the same as for Håkonshallen and, if you pay the full price for one museum, you get to see the other for half price.

Both museums are open from 10am until 4pm on weekdays and 12am to 3pm at weekends.

Not surprisingly, the Bergenser are proud of their heritage and they were reportedly furious when, during World War Two, Håkonshallen and the nearby Rosenkrantz Tower, a combined defence and residential tower built in the 1560s, were nearly levelled to the ground when a Dutch ship, the *Voorbode,* suddenly blew up in the harbour.

The explosion was heard 50 miles away. And it changed the city more than any of the other disasters, including numerous fires, that the city had endured. The ageing steamship docked in Bergen on April 16th, 1944 for engine repairs, on its way from Oslo to Kirkenes in the far north.

Although it was anchored in the harbour close to the town, few people took notice of what was apparently just another supply ship for the army of occupation. But the *Voorbode,* (which, if I'm not mistaken means 'forbidden'), was no ordinary supply ship; it was loaded to the gunnels with hundreds of tons of high explosives and 180,000 blasting caps, enough to destroy an appreciable part of the city.

That is precisely what it did when it exploded four days later, hurling parts of the ship an unbelievable *15 miles* from the town and killing or injuring more than 5,000 townspeople, its crew and dozens of Russian prisoner dock workers.

Two Norwegian marine engineers had been summoned to the ship on April 20th to assess the repair work necessary. On boarding it, they noticed smoke pouring from one of the coal bunkers, a sign of spontaneous combustion. They warned the ship's officers, who instead of acting to fight the impending fire, leapt onto the dock and ran as fast as they could away from the ship.

It just so happened that April 20th that year happened to be Hitler's 55th birthday and perhaps the Bergenser should not have been too surprised when the occupation authorities immediately blamed sabotage. However, the Bergenser knew otherwise.

To begin, no Norwegian resistance fighter would have ever blown up a ship at 8.39 am when the streets were full of people on their way to work. Nor would they ever have elected to destroy Håkonshallen.

The truth emerged after the war: the *Voorbode* had sailed with a false manifest, which was why it had been allowed to dock so close to the city in the first place. Incredibly, one of the ship's anchors still lies where it hit the ground on ***Fløyen*** mountain, some 300 metres or 900 feet higher, and more than a mile from where the ship had been docked.

A small park has been built around the anchor. If you stand there you can tell the true Bergenser among the many elderly who stroll by on their Sunday walks. They're the ones who doff their caps.

From Håkonshallen, continue walking along the quayside for 500 yards or so and you will come to Bergen's most famous landmark, ***Bryggen and the Hanseatic quarter.***

The quayside used to be called *Tyskebryggen,* the German Wharf, but after the Second World War it simply became known as Bryggen. The Wharf. This is a warren of gabled, wooden buildings and narrow alleyways, which from the mid-14th century was the hub of the powerful Hanseatic merchants' trading operations.

These merchants controlled a mercantile alliance which included more than 70 northern seaports, all trading favourably with each other and assisting each other in their military defence.

By the mid-16th century the Hanseatic League was in decline, although the last German merchant hung on in Bergen until 1764.

The original medieval buildings were mostly destroyed by fire in 1702 and replaced by high-gabled stone warehouses built in the same style. But a small section of timber buildings survived, and these are what you see today.

Nowadays, they are used for offices, restaurants, pubs, tourist shops, artists' studios and workshops for painters, weavers and other craftspeople. Many of these workshops and galleries are open to the public.

The buildings fronting the harbour (*photo on previous page)* are almost exclusively tourist shops today, bulging with colourful Norwegian sweaters, Viking paraphernalia (including the ubiquitous helmets with horns, which real Vikings never wore) and a plethora of trolls.

Incredible as it may seem, there are people in rural Norway who still believe that trolls exist!

Among these buildings are two museums, both of them excellent and well worth the visit.

The first is the **Hanseatic Museum** in a clearly signposted corner building at the end of the row. This gives you a good feeling for the way that life was lived here. It was a tough life, too! Strict rules dictated where people worked and lived. Trade was carried out at the front of the buildings, storage at the back.

Above were the merchant's office and living quarters, and above those the living quarters of the employees, all arranged by rank. So, above the merchants were the clerks and foremen, and above them the wharf hands. Finally, the last and least important, the house boys, whose life it has to be said must have been thoroughly miserable, and rather smelly given that they stank of fish and bathed only once a year.

Every activity in this hierarchical, all-male society was tightly controlled. Fraternisation with the local people was forbidden. Stiff fines were imposed for hundreds of offences, from swearing, waking up the master or singing at work. Perish the thought of it!

Sadly, the Hanseatic Museum is closed for six years until 2024 for restoration. However, it has relocated to **Schøtstuene (Hanseatic Assembly Rooms)** just behind the original museum.

Then there is **Bryggen Museum**, next to the SAS hotel, which lies just a few hundred yards on from Håkonshallen. This museum is cleverly built on top of excavations that began in 1955, when parts of Bryggen burned down.

The subsequent 13-year excavation uncovered more than 100,000 artefacts that give us a remarkable insight into medieval life in Bergen.

This museum is arguably the city's showpiece, with domestic implements, handicrafts, maritime objects and trade goods forming the basis of several excellent exhibits showing how people lived from the 12th century to the Middle Ages. It really is a fabulous exhibition.

Ticket prices and opening times are the same as the other museums.

Next, if, instead of turning right into the fish market, you keep going straight on, you'll see on your left a small street leading up to **Fløybanen, the funicular**

railway that takes you up to a lookout point 1,000 feet over the city.

If the weather is fine, you'll see some pretty stunning views. There's a café-restaurant and a large souvenir shop up there, so no problems about spending your money. But, of course, its the funicular itself and the views that make it worth while.

After descending the funicular, walk straight ahead to the end of the harbour and the ***Open-air fish market***.

If you are one of the few cruise passengers who speak Norwegian, strolling round it is like walking in and out of a continuous conversation, with sturdy fishmongers guarding solid-masonry tanks teeming with live cod or, in season, crawling with crustaceans.

To the Bergenser, a *fresh* fish or lobster is the one with the tail still flipping.

It really is a fantastic and fun place, and the displays of dressed crab, lobsters, fresh salmon and smoked salmon are not only mouth watering but also something of an art form.

One of the great joys of Bergen is buying a bag of prawns and eating them right there on the spot. The stalls even provide you with little pots of mustard dill sauce and mayonnaise.

Perhaps the tastiest of all the shellfish on offer is the Norwegian Red King Crab.

This magnificent individual only arrived in Norwegian waters in the 1960s.

Originally from the Barents Sea and probably related to the Alaskan Red King Crab, it was first introduced by Soviet scientists to boost the diet of the Murmansk population, many of whom were starving.

With legs that span up to six feet (1.8 metres) and with some weighing as much as 28lbs (12.7 kilos), fisherman can only handle each one individually.

Since being introduced to Murmansk waters, an entire army of these monsters have denuded the seabed from the Kola Peninsula coast to the crown of Norway.

These crabs are particularly rich in protein and also contain B12 vitamins (good for the brain) and selenium, an anti-oxidant.

They are also incredibly tasty with massive, juicy claws filled with white meat, but they are only available in season between October and December.

If you can get the timing right, for instance on a Christmas cruise, you might also be able to eat a dish not only of King Crab but also Skrei (pronounced *skray*).

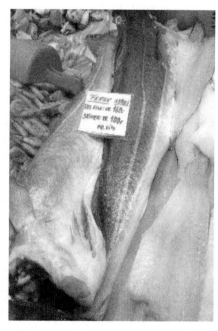

This is a teenage, muscular fish that swims down from the clear, cold waters of the Barents Sea to spawn off the Lofoten Islands.

Skrei is only fished from January to March, which is what makes the combination possible. It is deemed by leading chefs the world over to be the tastiest cod in the world.

When my wife and I first read about it in an airline magazine, we decided that we would make a meal of it our top priority.

That proved more difficult than we could ever have imagined because in winter, most restaurants do not serve Skrei until the evening. We tried at least half a dozen before we ended up in Dickens restaurant (*King Olav's Plass 4, Tel: +47 55 36 31 30*).

Here, too, we were told it was served only in the evenings, but when we explained that we were on a cruise ship leaving at 4 pm, the chef agreed to cook us a meal of skrei.

Served with boiled potatoes, a few mushy peas and carrots, it was the most exquisitely delicious fish dish we had ever tasted, glistening a brilliant white and flaking off at the merest nudge of a fork.

The Fish Market is also the location of the Tourist Information Office, which lies on the corner furthest from the Funicular railway above a couple of fish restaurants.

Surrounding the Fish Market, there are often ordinary market stalls offering clothes, ubiquitous baseball caps. belts and Norwegian souvenirs. There are also usually a couple of Sami people selling all things to do with reindeer – pelts, knives, wooden cups etc.

The end of the fish market marks the beginning of a large pedestrian shopping area at the entrance to which is the *Seamen's Monument,* a square plinth lined with statues of seafarers from Viking times to the 20th century.

Walking on through the pedestrian shopping area, it is hard to believe that during the Second World War, this was covered with tank blockades and Nazi troops.

If you walk to the end of the pedestrian area, marked by Dicken's Restaurant, then turn left down the hill, past the monument to the Norwegian violinist Ole Bull and cross the main road (which is where cruise shuttle buses park), you will come to *Festplassen (Festival Place)*, the venue for contemporary art installations and other festivities, and a large lake around which it is always a pleasure to walk.

Walking to the right of the lake, you will see the *Bergen Contemporary Art Museum*, also described as Bergen Art Hall or Code, one of Norway's largest contemporary art venues with screening rooms for multimedia, video art, theatre, electronic music and concerts. There is a café and the museum is open every day except Monday from 11am until 4pm. Tickets are a very reasonable NOK50 (£4.50, $5.85, €5.15) with a 50% reduction for students and seniors.

At the other end of the lake, still on the right hand side, is another museum known as *Kode 3,* which

includes a large collection of works by Edvard Munch and reflects the 'golden age' of Norwegian art spanning 150 years..

The museum is open at the same times as the Contemporary Art Museum. Tickets cost NOK 130 (£11.80, $15.20, €13.35) with concessions for students but not seniors.

Having reached the end of the lake, if you walk across to the other side, you might like to drop in at the main *Bergen railway station,* which was opened in 1913 four years after the inauguration of the 308-mile (496-km) Oslo to Bergen line.

This is said to be the highest mainline railway line in Europe, crossing the beautiful Hardanger plateau just over 4,000 feet (1,230 metres) above sea level.

Apart from being a major commercial centre, Bergen is also a significant centre of education with its university and several colleges, as well as being the cultural heart of the region, with an international Festival of Music and Art every Spring.

Music lovers from all over the world come to annual summer concerts at Edvard Grieg's home, known as *Troldhaugen,* located *at* Troldhaugvegen 65, Paradis, which is about six miles (10 km) or a 17-minute drive from Bergen city centre.

Close by is also *Grieghallen,* the Grieg Music Hall, renowned in Europe as the home of one of the world's oldest orchestras, the *Bergen Philharmonic,* which was founded in 1765.

So, music has, and still does, play an important role in the city's life. Grieg, incidentally, was a self-confessed misfit at his school in Bergen, where he was known as pupil no 139.

Troldhaugen is a pleasant but unassuming white clapboard house on a hill by a lake. It was the composer's home for the last 22 years of his life, although he spent much of that time abroad touring the concert halls of Europe.

Grieg was an immensely likeable man, much loved by all who knew him. Perhaps 'immense' is a misnomer because, in fact, he was only five-feet-five inches tall and looked not unlike Albert Einstein.

By all accounts, he was a modest man and once said that he made no pretensions of being in the same class as Beethoven, Mozart and Bach because, whereas their works were eternal, he said "I wrote for my day and generation."

Indeed, he was one of those rare composers who was actually appreciated during his lifetime. Hence, one of the rooms of his house is full of trophies, citations and honours, and a black Steinway piano he received as a present, all on show at Troldhaugen.

Grieg's life and times are exhaustively chronicled in the museum. However, the truth is that Grieg didn't compose much in the house itself. He preferred to walk down to the small log cabin by the waterfront. This hut is still standing, although it is now dwarfed by the modern 200-seater concert hall.

It is exactly as he left it, though, with notebooks on the table and the scores of Beethoven's concertos lying on the chair and the upright piano. So, visitors definitely get a very good feel for the man, his life and also his works there.

Grieg and his wife, Nina, who was an opera singer, are both buried at Troldhaugen in a very simple tomb in the side of a cliff. This is only couple of minutes' walks down the main footpath and not too many people go there, but it's a very beautiful spot and well worth it if you have the time.

Open every day (except 14 December-5th January), tickets cost NOK110 (£210, $12.80, €11.30). No

concession for seniors but students get in for half price.

Another attraction outside Bergen is the *Fantoft Stave Church* on the outskirts of a village rather immodestly called 'Paradise', a 16-minute, 8 km drive from Bergen. This rare stave church was originally built in Fortun in Sogn, a village near the end of the Sognefjord circa 1150.

It was moved to Fantoft near Bergen in 1882 but tragically burned down in 1992 as a result of arson. The church was rebuilt in 1997. The term 'stave', incidentally, refers to the huge posts that support it.

The church is privately owned and admission is charged to pay for its upkeep. Unfortunately, in 1992, it

was almost completely destroyed by yet another fire. However, during the past few years volunteers have worked flat out to rebuild it.

You can now see its many ingenious features, not least the ancient Viking shipbuilding techniques most clearly visible in the construction of the roof and in the carvings of serpents and dragons.

Fantoft is open from 15th May-15th September from 1030am-6pm. If you are travelling independently, tickets cost NOK 60 (£5.50, £7.00, €6.15).

Other attractions include the Buekorps *museum*, on the opposite side of the harbour from Bryggen. This depicts the 135-year history of the Buekorps, which is a kind of Boys' Brigade found only in Bergen and best known for their drill, usually with crossbows.

The Museum of Natural History has a giant octopus and a number of whale skeletons, and is said to house Norway's largest collection of 'natural objects'.

These are housed in the Botanical Garden, greenhouses and a Zoological Museum.

The latter curates both permanent and changing exhibitions with displays of a replica beaver dam, various scenes from the Arctic regions, penguins in Antarctica and wildlife from Africa.

The Botanical Garden boats 35,000 plants, 7,500 species and a 150-acre garden. Entry to the garden is free and all parts of the Natural History Museum are free on Thursdays.

Otherwise, the entry fee for adults is NOK 120 (£10.85, $14.00, €12.30) with half price for students and seniors.

So, there are any number of places to visit and things to see in Bergen. There is even a *Leprosy Museum* housed on the site of St. Jørgens Hospital for lepers at Kung Osscarsgate No. 59, a tribute to the doctors and scientists who have waged war on this terrible disease.

In the latter half of the 19th century, there were three leprosy hospitals in Bergen, in which medical staff cared for the largest number of patients in the world. St. Jørgens Hospital is the oldest of the three.

Leprosy is also known as Hansen's disease, named after Gerard Hansen, a Norwegian doctor who discovered the leprosy bacillus in 1873.

Tickets cost NOK 100 (£9.05, $11.65, €10.25 and there are daily tours between 22nd June and 18th August in English at 11 am at an extra cost of NOK 30.

Finally, and just to reassure you, there is absolutely no chance of contracting leprosy by visiting the hospital.

On that happy note, it is time to head back to your ship and sail for your next port of call.

***

FLÅM, NAERØYFJORD & GUDVANGEN

Flåm lies at the head of the 29-kilometre (18-mile) long Aurlandsfjord, itself a southern spur of the 204-km (127-mile) long Sognefjord, the maximum depth of which is 1,308 metres or 4,291 feet. This compares with Scotland's highest mountain, which is 1,345 metres or 4,413 ft high. Put Ben Nevis on the seabed and you would see only the top 122-feet (37-metres).

Like Bergen, Flåm is one of the most visited ports in Norway, with some 400,000 tourists and cruise passengers from approximately 160 cruise ships each year.

To cater for them all, there are five hotels, one of which has 122 rooms, six junior suites, 17 historic rooms with antique furniture, an historic tower suite and 12 'America' rooms with balconies.

There are large restaurants, huge souvenir shops, a museum and not a great deal else, except for the one thing that everyone comes for, which is the *Flåm railway*.

Described by Lonely Planet as the world's most beautiful train journey, arguably an exaggeration, the Flåm railway is certainly one of the world's steepest on a 'normal' track.

The hour-long journey takes you up an average gradient of 1 in 18 rising some 863.5 metres (2,840 ft) over a distance of 20 kilometres (12 miles) and through 20 tunnels, four of which are 'water' tunnels.

Spiralling in and out of the mountain it is not for anyone suffering from even the mildest acrophobia (vertigo).

For those who don't, it's a breath-taking ride. It begins with a small museum at Flåm railway station, which highlights the audacious engineering skills of the men who designed and built it.

The idea of a railway from Flåm was first spawned in 1871.

That plan was to link up with the Bergen–Oslo railway. Not renowned for making instant decisions, the Norwegian parliament decided 37 years later that the line should be constructed with Myrdal, near Voss, as its summit destination.

Even then, there must have been some concern about the construction, whether it should be a rack and pinion track or a cable track, for instance, because construction didn't begin for another 16 years, in 1924.

The driver's cab

That the railway was built at all was a near miracle! Of the 20 tunnels, 18 had to be carved out by hand. This was an incredibly difficult task, not least because it would take one labourer a month of dynamiting and then hacking away at the rock just to advance one metre.

Blasting and clearing the tunnels was calculated to take as many as 180-man hours per metre. Not surprisingly, construction of the line took another 16 years.

The finances of the Norwegian government were partly responsible for this. At the time, the economy fluctuated considerably and the knock-on effect of that was that there was only enough money to pay 120 labourers. In more prosperous years, as many as 220 were employed.

In April, 1940, the Germans occupied Norway and with five kilometres of track still to be laid, insisted that construction continue apace.

The line was finally opened for freight four months later, in August, 1940, initially using steam-powered locomotives. A year later, after the locomotives had been fitted with engine-powered brakes rather than manual ones, the line opened for passengers.

The Germans supplied electric locomotives and a power plant at the Kjosfossen waterfalls. However, Norwegian resistance fighters blew up the plant, so the line was not electrified until 1947.

By 1953, nearly 120,000 passengers were travelling from Flåm to Myrdal each year, five times as many passengers as had been anticipated originally. Today, that figure is well over half a million, with as many as 5,000 passengers a day when cruise ships arrive in port.

A gentle start to the journey –
Flåm Valley and the Kjosfossen
falls.

View from the top

For tourists who do not have a head for heights, a walk along Flåm Valley is invigorating, beautiful and rewarding.

Just walk to the end of the quay, to the right of the Fretheim Hotel and follow the road with the railway on your left and along the banks of the salmon river.

This is a delightful walk, the air gloriously fresh.

Only in rural Norway, will you see the post boxes so richly decorated!

Salmon and trout fishing were the original lure for visitors to Flåm. English salmon lords would come here with a large entourage of followers between July and September. You can buy fishing licences at the tourist information office. Or perhaps just walk gingerly along the wooden walkways at the side of the river?

About two miles (3 kms) out of town on the river bank, is *Flåm Church (Flåm Kyrke)*, a small wooden church dating back to 1667.

Open to visitors in the summer, the church was decorated during the 18th century with what, in terms of church art, are unique pictures of animals and trees.

The altar, however, dates to 1681.

Seating 160 parishioners, the church replaced an older stave church.

Flåm church is one of about 60 17th century churches remaining in Norway and is in such superb condition it is difficult to conceive that it is 350 years old.

Returning to the village centre, you can see the opening to Norway's second longest tunnel – the 7.1-mile (11,428 metre) route to the village of Gudvangen.

Aurlandsfjord is a little like a three-pronged garden fork with Flåm at the end of the right-hand prong and Gudvangen at the end of the left-hand fork. The tunnel links them both.

A far better way to see the villages is to take a tourist boat to Gudvangen via *Naerøyfjord* (although that may not be necessary as

many cruise ships cruise Naerøyfjord to Gudvangen, anyway).

Listed on UNESCOs World Heritage sites, Naerøyfjord is often described as the most beautiful and wildest arm of the Sognefjord. It is certainly one of the narrowest (Trollfjord in northern Norway has that distinction) and Geirangerfjord is arguably just as beautiful and wild.

However, the wonderful thing about Naerøyfjord is that it doesn't matter what the weather is like – it is beautiful always – moody and melancholy sometimes, yes, but always visually stunning, lined with snow-capped mountains, huge waterfalls, tiny houses on the clifftops and miniscule hamlets.

Usually, only the tourist boats actually stop at **Gudvangen**, which boasts a 30-bedroom hotel with a restaurant-cafeteria for 250 people and an outdoor terrace for 200 people.

***

FLORØ

Not many cruise ships come to Florø and those that do tend to be smaller ships for which this delightful fishing town, nestling amongst a multitude of tiny islands, is able to provide facilities.

In many ways, Florø, is even more picturesque, not to mention idyllic, than Skudeneshavn *(page. 191-192)*. It is the westernmost town in Scandinavia (west of Brussels and Amsterdam) and was founded by royal decree in 1860 as a port of lading, which is to say a port where goods are put on a ship and documented.

With a population of approximately 8,700 inhabitants, this enchanting town was built on the site of a farm called Flóra, which in Old Norse meant 'fast flowing stream'. (Later, the 'a' was replaced by 'ø', which means island).

Like many towns along the southwestern coast of Norway, Florø existed primarily because of the abundant herring fisheries, which are represented in the town's coat of arms by three herring.

Today, fishing remains a major source of income, although the town has become more dependent on shipbuilding, service industries and as a supply town for the oil industry.

Not that these industries dominate the town, which has retained its small-town, village atmosphere. In 1998, Florø was designated an 'Environmental City' by the

Norwegian Minister of the Environment for its environmental consciousness and care. To describe Florø as a city, however, is like describing a peanut as a potato.

This is a place to wander round. There is only one main street – Strandgatan – which is lined with a good selection of shops, many of them selling high quality products.

 There are surprises at every corner and it evident that many of the residents possess an artistic bent. On one corner, a bicycle with a basket of flowers and three herring 'balloons' dangling from the handlebars. On another a pot of flowers with stylised glass tropical fish.

Such small details and the general 'feel' of Florø are a little reminiscent of Bar Harbour in Maine. Another bonus with this town is that your ship will be berthed within yards of the town centre.

Perhaps the best possible excursion would be to take the 'Bybus' – the Town bus, which is a panoramic tour in itself. As somebody said: "The ship would have charged us $100 for this".

In fact, this is just a regular scheduled bus that drives all around the town and its environs and is the most pleasant way to pass an hour. The countryside is stunning!

Another brilliant way to spend the afternoon is to take the ferry to Barekstad and Fanø, which leaves at 2.30pm. This is arguably the very best way to absorb Norwegian coastal life. You can choose to go to the northern islands in the archipelago or the southern. My wife and I chose the northern islands.

As we stood on the afterdeck, the captain, Rune Aldeholm, asked: "Are you English tourists?" I answered in the affirmative and expected him to say: "Well, you can't stand here!"

Instead, he said: "Would you and your wife like to accept my invitation to come up on the bridge for the rest of the trip. There is a much better view from up there".

It was magical! The coastal scenery was wonderful with rugged rocks and islets. The crew were friendly, brewing us coffee – and the captain took us to a tiny wooden house on an islet off Store Batalden, where he told us his mother had been born.

In the southern islands, the lighthouse on the island of Kinn is worth seeing.

The Coastal Museum is situated on Brendøyvegen, an idyllic coastal site a 35-minute walk from the town centre. (Or you can take the town bus).

The museum showcases three exhibition buildings connected by a network of paths and bridges. There is a large outdoor area with farmhouses and fishing villages relocated here, including a 17th century salting shack used for curing herring, which you can smell to this day.

The area includes nature trails, picnic areas with grazing goats in summer and rowing boats for hire. This is a museum ideal for children, too – even on rainy days they can go crabbing.

(You just lie on your stomach at the end of a pier or on a bridge, tie clothes peg to a long piece of string, attach a stone to weigh it down and within minutes you can haul up a crab!)

Exhibitions focus on the natural and cultural history of the coastal environs. It has one of the largest exhibitions on oil industry activity in Norway, a collection of boats and a display about commerce. There is also a shop and a café.

Opening times vary but are usually from 10 am to 3pm and longer in summer. Tickets are NOK 80 (£7.20, $9.30, €8.20) for adults, NOK 50 (£4.50, $5.80, €5.10) for seniors and students, and NOK 30 (£2.70, $3.50, €3.10) for children aged between seven and 18 years.

***

FREDRIKSTAD

Renowned as the best-preserved fortress town in Northern Europe, Fredrikstad is the gateway to, and lies on the eastern shore of, the Oslo fjord, 56 miles (90 kms) or an hour and 15-minute drive from the capital.

During the Northern Seven Year's War at the time of the 16th century Danish-Norwegian Union, the Swedish army torched the ancient town of Sarpsborg, nine miles (15 kilometres) north of today's Fredrikstad.

As a result, in 1567, the Danish king, Fredrik II, gave the order to build a fortified city with moats and high earth ramparts to act as a defensive barrier against the Swedes – and being a modest man, in 1569 he named it Fredrikstad after himself.

The zigzag moat and ramparts proved highly successful in defending the city, which was never captured or placed under siege.

Originally, the city depended on fishing and agriculture for its existence, but later, in the mid-1800s, it relied more on timber exports and by 1870, industrialists had built several steam-powered sawmills along the river banks.

Eventually, timber exports declined and shipbuilding came to the fore, and remained the principal source of income until the late 1980s.

Today, the city's income is derived main from light industry and some chemical manufacturing plants.

During the 21st century, the city has twice hosted the Tall Ship's Race, in 2005, when it was the final port of call and in 2019 when it was the starting point, both occasions attracting thousands of spectators to the port.

Fredrikstad, together with its neighbouring town, Sarpsborg, now form the fifth largest city in Norway with a population of 136,117. This is made up of Fredrikstad's population of 80,977 and that of Sarpsborg's 55,140.

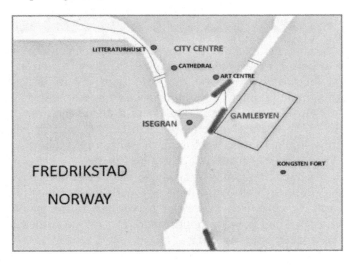

The city is essentially divided into three parts – the Old Town (Gamlebyen), the City centre and Isegran.

If you imagine that the river Glomma splits into the form of the letter 'Y', the modern part of the city is located between the left and right 'arms' of the letter.

The Old Town is situated on the right-hand arm, close to the stem, and the island of Isegran is opposite to it in the centre of the river.

Cruise ships approach the town through the archipelago of the Hvaler Islands, which consist of some 833 islands and skerries.

Much of this archipelago is designated as Norway's first national (Ytre Hvaler) marine park and given that this is said to be the sunniest (or one of the sunniest) regions in Norway, it is a magnet for holidaymakers keen to go fishing, swimming, sailing and sunbathing.

There are several beaches reasonably close to the town but Scandinavians are more used to lying and picnicking on granite rocks that slope gently down to the sea.

Named after the plural word for whale, the islands are said to resemble a pod of minke whales when the sun sets behind them, casting them into deep shade.

The Hvaler islands, approximately 13 miles (22 kms) south of Fredrikstad, are easily reached along Route 108 in 30 minutes.

Alternatively, you can take one of several island-hopping ferries there.

The rewards for the journey are fabulous hiking trails through the birch forests, isolated coves, kayaking, lunching out on fresh seafood or visiting the *Hvaler Coastal Museum,* the only museum of its kind in Østfold county. It can be found at Nordgården, Dypedal on Spjærøy island (also accessible on Route 108)

Known as the Island of Culture, Spjærøy existed on the proceeds of agriculture, fishing, piloting and shipping until the 1800s, when a stone cutting industry became more dominant.

The coastal museum, surrounded by an attractive garden and orchard, covers it all.

It is open between June 23rd and August 19th from 10 noon until 4pm. Admission is NOK 60 (£5.45, $6.70, €6.05)

Another island is Hankø, once a hunting ground for a local lord, now owned by Princess Martha of Norway and her family. Accessible by boat or ferry from Hankø Sound (Hankøsundet), the island was propelled to fame when sulphurous mud was discovered there in the 1870s.

In no time, it had become a spa. In 1877, the owners of a sanitarium converted it into the HankøFjord & Spa Hotel.

Then, at the turn of the century, local people introduced fallow deer from Denmark, hare and pheasants, so that the hunting tradition could be continued.

In 1930, King Olav, doubtless attracted by the peace and tranquility the island offers, bought a holiday home there.

Most cruise ships berth at one of the quays along the stem and right-hand arm of the 'Y-shaped river junction, often right next to *Gamlebyen (The Old Town)*, a grid of charming cobbled streets and wooden and baroque houses that are home to about 350 residents.

Here, you can wander along the ramparts, sit on a bench and absorb the history, take photographs of the goats or relax over a cappuccino or a bottle of wine in one of the many cafés and restaurants.

Or you can explore the boutiques, galleries and museums. If you arrive in Fredrikstad on a Saturday, you also have the option of pottering around a popular flea market.

The Old Town is also the venue for several of Fredrikstad's main attractions. For example, *Fredrikstad Museum*, located at Tøihusgaten No. 41, has a permanent exhibition giving an insight into the history of the city from its foundation in 1567 until the present day.

The museum is housed in a former military warehouse dating back to 1776 and which once was the largest building in Norway.

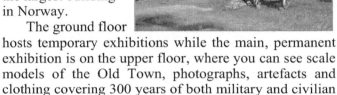

The ground floor hosts temporary exhibitions while the main, permanent exhibition is on the upper floor, where you can see scale models of the Old Town, photographs, artefacts and clothing covering 300 years of both military and civilian life.

There are costumed guides and a unique 'history bar' known as Bar 1567 where visitors sit at a bar (no, drinks are not served here, only history) watching images on a screen that tell of the big events and how, after war, fire and crisis, rebuilt their homes.

As the museum claims, "you are sucked into the story in a way you have never experienced before'.

Opening hours: Monday-Friday 9am-5pm, Saturday 10am-3pm, Sunday 11am-3pm. (From September onwards 9am-4pm, closed weekends. Times change from year to year).

Admission is NOK 35 (£3.10, $3.90, €3.50). Please note that there have been some complaints in the past that there are little or few information captions in English. Museum comments say this is now being addressed.)

The ramparts of the Old Town also enclose a thoroughly entertaining *Model Train Centre*, located at Voldgaten No. 8.

This is a fabulous display described as the largest model railway in Scandinavia, which comes highly recommended for all ages.

Here, enthusiasts have created a miniature landscape that covers more than 4,300 square feet (400 square metres) and through which 35 locomotives haul passenger and goods trains along more than one-and-a-quarter miles (two kilometres) of track.

What makes this display so extraordinarily impressive is the exquisite detail with moulded mountains, houses, hotels, farms, bridges, viaducts, fields of sheep, not to mention city squares and markets filled with people.

The enthusiasts have even built a replica of the Old Town, complete with ramparts. A neat touch was to put the control room for the computerised railway into a life-sized model of a real Norwegian locomotive.

Built on a scale of 1:87 with a 2.0-gauge track, the railway is open from June 16-August 16, Monday-Friday 11am-4pm, Saturday 11am-4pm, Sunday 12 noon-4pm. Admission NOK 50 (£.4.55, $5.60, €5.00).

About 500 yards/metres southeast of the Old Town is **Kongsten Fort**, built between 1682 and 1685 as an added defence on the most exposed approach to Fredrikstad.

This standalone fortress, perched on a rocky hillock, has protected the Norwegian border for some 500 years. It came under attack on several occasions but never succumbed and today stands proudly with stunning views to the southeast across flat agricultural and forestland to Halden and the Swedish border, about 25 miles (40 kilometres) away.

In its prime, the fort was populated with as many as 150 soldiers and 20 cannons. The only concern was whether, if it came under artillery fire, the rock face would be blown away, taking the fort with it.

Gradually, the fort's military importance receded, although it was not until the turn of the 20th century that it was finally abandoned. As an addendum, in 1985, the fort's 300th anniversary, a special stamp was issued with an image of the fortress.

There is no museum and therefore no admission fee to the fort, but it is worth a visit to see the ramparts, bastions, casemate, commander's house and powder magazine, not to mention the views of Fredrikstad and its environs.

The Old Town's first church, **Østra Fredrikstad Church**, located at the junction of Kirkegaten and Voldportgaten. is the seventh church to be built on the site. The first, a wooden church built in 1580, burned down – as did the other six, the last of them in 1764.

At that juncture, the city fathers sensibly decided to build a more solid edifice in brick and stone, which was inaugurated in September 1779 and can accommodate 650 worshippers.

One of the great attractions about Fredrikstad is that, although the city is divided into three sections, ferries connect each of them – and there is no charge, so you can use them for a free river tour of the city – and to enjoy a walk along the quayside promenade of the inner city.

Crossing the river from the Old Town to the Cicignon stop (left bank of the right arm on the 'Y'), the first attraction you come to is the ***Østfold Art Centre (Kunstsenter)***, located at Ferjestedsveien No. 5B.

Housed in an elegant and distinctive 19th century mansion painted brilliant white with a dark black roof, and situated in parkland close to the ferry quay, the centre is managed by artists who stage regular, temporary exhibitions with many of the works for sale.

Focusing on contemporary art, exhibitions cover paintings, sculpture, visual art and ceramics and conceptual art.

There is a shop and café for visitors and workshops for children. It is open from 12 noon to 5pm and there is no admission fee.

Although the city centre is as modern as any other city you would find in Norway, its charm lies in the open parks and along the waterfront.

It is on the promenade that you will find the *House of Literature (Litteraturhuset)* located at Storgata 11 (on the right bank of the left arm of the 'Y').

A large modern cube of a building that opened in January 2013 after fire destroyed a large area of the city, this house of culture is dedicated to the written word.

That said, the curators also host several live events, discussions and meetings where local people can, for instance, tackle local politicians face to face about local issues.

Both national and international speakers, not least Fay Weldon, Nuruddin Farah and John Dickie have attracted large audiences and in the six years since its conception, there have been more than 1,400 open events attended by more than 165,000 people.

The House of Literature is not exactly a tourist attraction in the usual sense, but there is a good café and restaurant there, and you may be lucky enough to see one of the many TED-style seminars, art exhibitions and readings.

There is no entrance fee and it is open from 10am until late Monday to Saturday and from 12 noon to 6pm on Sundays.

A little further downstream at Riddervoldsgate No.5, the 230-foot (70-metre) tower and copper spire of *Fredrikstad Cathedral (Domkirke)* rise above parkland dotted with sculptures.

With space for 1,100 people, it is an impressive Gothic building built with brick in the form of a Latin cross.

First consecrated in 1880 as a parish church, it is best known for its stained-glass windows by Emanuel Vigeland, an accomplished Norwegian religious artist who also has works in the cathedrals of Aarhus in Denmark, Lund in Sweden and Stavanger in Norway.

Apart from the obvious attractions, Fredrikstad is a city for meandering and there is more than enough to see and do for cruise passengers who are likely to spend only one day here.

Other attractions out of town include *Hans Nielsen Hauge's Memorial Museum* at No. 39 on the road named after him near Rolvsøy. (The Tourist Office will provide further directions).

Hauge was a perplexing, itinerant Lutheran preacher whose books spawned the gender-equal Haugean Movement.

This semi-secret group held casual and unsanctioned religious meetings in factories around the country, despite them having been banned, thus challenging the Church of Norway's authority.

The museum can be visited by appointment in advance by telephoning: +47 69 33 54 72.

A less enigmatic Norwegian was the polar explorer, Roald Amundsen, whose birthplace was a farm on the outskirts of Sarpsborg,

Roald Amundsen's birthplace is situated at Framveien No. 1659, on the banks of the River Glomma. It was here at the family farm that he first developed his yearning for adventure and exploration. He took an avid interest in the 17 sailing ships that belonged to his family's shipping company and which were moored just below the farm, now a museum.

The museum building is said to be one of the best-preserved houses in Norway and contains not only period furniture but also many relics and souvenirs from Amundsen's expeditions to the Northwest Passage, over the North Pole and to the South Pole.

The museum is open from July 24th-August 25th, from 11am-5pm, Wednesday to Sunday. There is no entrance fee.

For those seeking to spend the day relaxing on a beach, the best (Blue Flag) sandy beach is *Foton Beach*, about six miles (10 kilometres) southwest of Fredrikstad. This is essentially a sandy bay surrounded by smooth rocks sloping gently into the water. At sunset, these seem to glow a gorgeous pink colour.

The water quality and amenities are superb, with a volleyball court, wooden pier with bathing ladders and a multi-level diving board. There are also several hiking trails in the area

A new service building with refreshments and snacks has accessible toilets and there is also a covered way to a separate bathing ramp for the disabled.

Finally, for visitors who may have been to Fredrikstad before, the towns of Sarpsborg and Halden, both rich in history and surrounded by glorious countryside, are easily accessible by bus in about 30 minutes.

Aside from that, there is also the possibility of a full day's excursion to Oslo, but whatever you choose to do, this part of Norway is full of history, culture, old and new, and unless it is pouring with rain and brimstone, you are bound to have a great time.

***

OLDEN

Olden is a pleasant village at the head of Nordfjord populated by a mere 500 or so people. It has become a major cruise destination with more than 60 ships arriving each year.

They dock a ten-minute walk from the village centre, opposite a souvenir shop. The village has the usual shops, outlets, post office and café's, and there are two churches, the Old and the New. These are the main, if not the only attractions in the village and its immediate surroundings.

The Old Church was built in 1759 and replaced a stave church dating back to the 1300s.

The stave church was demolished in 1746 and in turn replaced by a wooden church which apparently blew down in a gale 11 years later. Timbers from the stave church were saved and used for the pews and pew doors in the current Cruciform church, which is built on the five squares of a Greek cross.

There are very few of these churches in West Norway, despite the fact that they are able to resist strong winds because of their shape.

One curious aspect of the church is that men always sat on the right-hand side and women on the left. The men's pews are adorned with hat racks known as *'krekser'*, made from the tops of young birch trees with the bark and some, but not all branches removed.

One of the hat racks bears the date 1672, probably carved by a local farmer as each farmer's family had their own gated pew.

A strange picture in Olden Old Church shows the town's elders, all of whom look a little like Santa Claus's helpers in their red floppy hats.

Nowadays, villagers worship in the New Church, which was built in 1934. Nonetheless, occasional services are still held in the Old Church on Independence Day (17th May) and on other special occasions.

Although the walk out of town, following the glacial river that flows down from the

Briksdal Glacier is not listed as an attraction, it is a delightful walk along a path lined with bushes that are laden with red currents glistening against the chalky green colour of the turbulent river.

The path eventually takes you to the lake known as Løken, which means 'The Onion', so named because of its shape.

From time to time, the water on the lake is mirror still and if you take a photograph, it is difficult to tell afterwards which are the mountains and which are the reflections.

This is also sometimes true for Nordfjord opposite to the cruise berth.

Olden's main claim to fame is that it is the gateway to the ***Briksdal Glacier*** and most, if not all, cruise ship sell their own excursions there.

Back in 1999, you used to be able to stand right up against the ice front, or snout as it is known. Sadly, that is no longer possible because the glacier has retreated several hundred metres.

There is nothing unusual about this; glaciers retreat and advance all the time. The only question is whether the cause here is climate change. There is no answer to that question, but what is certain is that the scenery remains unchanged.

On this excursion, wherever you go there is gentle, undulating farmland, steep grassy slopes, mirror

reflective lakes, rushing rivers, spectacular mountains and waterfalls spilling 10,000 litres of glacial water a second.

This is one of the few places where the much over-used word 'awesome' is truly relevant. It is impossible not to be struck by the magnificence of the *Jostedal National Park* and be 'awe-struck' by the mountain and glacial scenery.

This is Nature at its most superlative and, as always in such circumstances, it reduces visitors to a marvelling, respectful silence.

Kleivafossen, spilling 10,000 litres of glacial meltwater a second.

Your excursion will take you past Løken Lake along narrow roads and through equally narrow tunnels to Briksdal, where the mountains rise so steeply above you that you cannot help but leave with an aching neck!

There is a restaurant and large tourist shop and restaurant at the head of the glacier. Here you can buy Olden water, which is to say 100 per cent clean mineral taken from the glacier and bottled on site actually underneath the glacier.

The water is marketed as being thousands of years old – but still has a 'Best Before' date stamp!

***

ÅLESUND

    If you were to sum up Ålesund in a sentence, it would be: Renowned for its art nouveau buildings, Ålesund is Norway's largest fishing harbour which is surrounded by stunning coastal views, islands and snow-capped mountains.

    The town dates from the ninth century when Rollo the Ganger built a castle here. Ålesund, however, did not officially become a town until 1848. In those days, the buildings were all wooden and in 1904, fire aggravated by gale force winds destroyed almost the entire town, miraculously killing only one person but causing more than 10,000 others to lose their homes.

Kaiser Wilhelm of Germany, who had been to Norway on vacation many times, sent four warships laden with temporary shelters and barracks to help the rescue effort.

The town was then rebuilt, but this time with stone, brick and mortar in the Jugend style. Today, Ålesund is the commercial centre for the county of Møre (*pronounced 'mur-y as in murky*) and Romsdal. It has retained its Art Nouveau charm with a myriad of turrets, spires and Jugend ornamentation.

Not surprisingly, Ålesund is home to the ***Norwegian Centre of Art Nouveau Architecture***, a museum and information centre which mounts exhibitions telling the story of the fire and all things Jugend.

Fortunately, as most of the military combat during the Second World War took place at sea, the town was largely spared the ravages of the German occupation.

It was, however, often described as 'Little London' because of the exploits of Resistance fighters in the area, many of whom took advantage of established escape routes to England and Scotland.

Built on two islands linked by bridges, the town itself has a population of some 48,000 with another 5,500 residents in the greater urban area.

As always, the best way to see the town is to walk round it, get lost a little and perhaps follow a route on the tourist map. (***The Tourist Information Office*** is in Skateflukaia at the far end of the inland channel at the junction with Skansegata, Tel: +47 70 16 34 30).

From the quayside, the best route is to walk on the right-hand side of the channel known as Ålesundet (which means 'The Eel Sound') and keep going until you are opposite the end of the left-hand island. This is where you will find the best photographic shots.

After that you would need to retreat the way you came for a while and then head into the centre of the town to see the main Jugend district.

There are several museums in Ålesund. One of the main ones is ***Sunnmøre Museum***, an open-air museum with a collection of nearly 60 old houses and boats, including replicas of Viking ships. Here you can learn all about the cultural and architectural history of Sunnmøre, the district in which Ålesund lies.

The 50-acre museum is located a five-minute taxi ride from the downtown area and covers the population's life and work from the Stone Age to the present day.

The museum is open from every day between 10 am and 4pm from May to September, 10am -3pm Tuesday to Friday and 12-4pm on Sunday between October and April.

Tickets NOK 80 (£7.15, $9.40, €8.25) for adults, NOK 60 (£5.35, $7.05, €6.20) for seniors and students.

Ålesundsmuseet (Ålesund Museum) covers the city's emergence as a seafaring town to the great fire and the German occupation. It is located on the hill called Museumshaugen, with great views of the city and surrounding islands.

Built in 1919, it retains the character of one of the larger private houses of that era and is a charming place to visit. An impressive model of the town depicts the town in 1898 – in other words before the fire. There are also displays from the German occupation, an old dentist's operating theatre and much else besides.

In the adjacent park is a statue of Rollo, as he is

 known today. His real name was Hrolf in Old Norse, a Viking chieftain who lived between circa 846 and 930AD. He became the first ruler of Normandy, having shed the mantle of King Harald the First of Norway and sailed off to raid Scotland, England and France.

He was later known as Gaange ('The Walker) Hrólfr, the former derived from the Old Norse verb 'gaa' (*pronounced gaw or gore)* which means to walk. (It still does in both Swedish and Norwegian). This was because rather overdid the feasting and became so large and heavy that he could no longer ride a horse.

Eventually, his three times great grandson became William the First, Conqueror of England.

The park lies close by, and this is the starting point for anyone wishing to walk up the 418 steps to the Aksla Viewpoint.

Opening times for the museum vary from 10am-4pm Tuesday to Friday and 12-4pm Sunday (Mondays closed). Tickets NOK 60. Seniors NOK 50 (£4.45, $5.85, €5.15)

Mount Aksla Viewpoint (Fjellstua) dominates the town. There is a café and a restaurant, and the panoramic views of the town, the archipelago and the Sunnmøre Alps are fabulous.

You can either drive up or walk from the town park up the 418 steps (or 446 steps depending on the route) to the top.

Those who have done the climb say it is easy with asphalt pathways, steps and plenty of benches on which to rest and enjoy the views. Those suffering from even mild acrophobia will take one look and say 'No Way!'

The *Art Nouveau Centre (Jugendstilsenteret)* is located in the old Swan Pharmacy and offers an insight into the Jugend style with authentic interiors and artefacts as well as temporary exhibitions. It is an educational centre.

The museum is situated on Apotekergata 16 (Tel: +47 70 10 49 71.) and is open every day between 10 am and 5 pm from May until September and from 11am to 4pm from October to April. It is closed, like most museums in Norway, on Mondays.

A ten-minute drive out of Ålesund on the E136 is the *Atlantic Sea-Park,* also known as the *Norwegian Aquarium.*

Built into the coastal landscape, with a spectacular view to the Atlantic, the museum's main attractions are the large unfiltered seawater tanks, which showcase life along this part of the Atlantic coast.

Each day at 1pm, divers enter the largest tank to hand feed the fish. The penguins have to wait for another hour and a half, at 2.30pm.

There is a great water park for children and there are harbour seals in the largest seal pool in Europe. In fact, it was here that we first took Selik, the seal mentioned in *Summer with Selik* on page 128 onwards.

Another popular excursion is to the islands of *Giske and Gudøy.* Giske, said to be where Rollo was born, is an island community connected to Ålesund by two long tunnels under the sea. It has a population of approximately 8,200,

For those who have been to Ålesund before, or who just want to get away to the countryside, this is a fabulous tour with mountains blanketed with snow even in summer, fishing villages, nature reserves, sandy beaches and burial mounds dating some 8,000 years back.

Giske, about ten kilometres (6.2 miles) northwest of Ålesund, is also the location of one of Norway's most remarkable churches, being the only church in Norway built with white marble.

Unfortunately, today the exterior of the church is covered with chalk and the interior with plaster. Quite why is anybody's guess.

Nobody knows where the white marble came from but it clearly arrived by boat.

Originally built as a private chapel for a powerful noble family in the 12th century, the church has been refurbished several times and the interior was created in the mid-18th century. It is still very much in use today.

Apart from being the supposed birthplace of Rollo, Giske is also said to be the place where Harald Fairhair (also known as Harald Finehair), having vowed that he would not cut his hair until he had unified the Kingdom of Norway, finally did so.

The island of *Godøy* is another opportunity to immerse yourself in the glorious freshness of the Norwegian west coast.

The focal point here is *Alnes Lighthouse*, a listed wooden building from 1876 that is still in use today.

At its base, there is a small café selling homemade cakes and traditional foods from the area. It is open year-round and there is also an art gallery featuring watercolours and sketches by a locally famous artist.

This tour usually also includes a trip up to the Mount Aksla viewpoint.

Almost all ships run this excursion, but if you prefer to do it independently, you can take bus number 658. The bus which stops at Giske and goes on to Godøy, runs every half hour at peak times and once an hour at other times. Check the return times with the driver. (Please also check the bus number is correct. They do sometimes change the numbers!)

Ålesund is also one of the great sailaways as your ship glides out of the port surrounded by the high mountains.

As you sail out, you will almost certainly want to return another time because once you've experienced the Norwegian west coast, it's in your blood!

***

GEIRANGER AND TROLLSTIGEN

Listed on UNESCOs World Heritage site since 2005 and lying more than 100 kilometres (60 miles) inland, Geirangerfjord is the 3rd biggest cruise ship port in Norway, with as many as 180 ships calling here during the summer season.

It is an anchorage port with three to four anchorage positions, depending on the ship's tonnage and if you feel somewhat overwhelmed by the wonderful scenery, you may well be more overwhelmed by the number of tourists during the May to September season.

At least 350,000 passengers arrive in cruise ships, but the total number of tourists is around 800,000 with some estimates claiming the number is as high as one million. That's a lot of people for a village with only 215 residents!

The principal reason for Geiranger's popularity is that Geirangerfjord is arguably 'among the most scenically outstanding fjord area on the planet', as one website describes it.

The first cruise ship arrived in 1869, just two years after the first guest house was built and the one thing its passengers wanted was transport.

The population then comprised farmers and their families, so transport was a good source of income for them; back in 1910, there were nearly 40 horse owners, who four years later were operating 'taxi' services with more than 80 horse-drawn carriages.

Later, the farmers turned to cars, some of them nine seaters. Just prior to the Second World War, there were as many as 60 of them operating up and down the surrounding mountains.

Some of these vintage vehicles are still on display at the Hotel Union.

Today, although there are taxi services available, you may well find it impossible to find one!

That means walking, which is by far the best way to see Geiranger and its environs, anyway.

Geiranger itself boasts a plethora of cafes, restaurants, tourist shops and a couple of museums. Once you have made your way through these, a gentle walk along the flat is along the left-hand side of the fjord (facing away from Geiranger centre) to Homlong.

Along the way you will see the **Eagle's Highway** across the fjord.

This is the road over the mountains to Eidsdal and Trollstigen (The Troll's Highway).

The Eagle's Highway comprises eleven hairpin turns rising to 2,030 ft (620 metres) above fjord level. Its highest bend offers spectacular views

of Geiranger and Geirangerfjord.

If you carry on walking to Homlong, you will see evidence of rock slides, ponies, wildflowers, a very pleasant area with picnic tables and tourist holiday chalets, and superb views back to Geiranger and its mountain background.

Another more popular walk is past the modern Hotel Geiranger and up the hill with the waterfall and rushing river on your right, and on to ***Geiranger church***, which affords magnificent views of the fjord.

The graveyard here is fascinating because behind every gravestone is a story of a remarkable people – the clifftop farmers of Geiranger, who lived lives of extreme hardship, often having to tether their children to their houses because of the 1,000 ft (610 metre) drop into the fjord.

In most cases, every plank of wood, every iron pot or stove and even the odd horse or pig had to be carried up on the backs of the clifftop farmers. It is one of the most extraordinary stories of our times.

These people and their lifestyle, accompanied by maps showing the location of each farm, are described in a separate booklet, *The Cruise Passenger's Guide to the Fjord People of Geiranger,* which is available at www.samhallbooks.com and on Amazon.com both as an eBook and paperback.

After visiting the church, carry on up the road to the **Union Hotel** and the **Norwegian Fjord Centre** where you can learn how the landscape here was created and how the local people lived.

This fascinating visit is well worth spending an hour of your day and is open from 10 am -3pm in the winter season and longer in the summer. Entrance fees are NOK 130 (£12.00, $15.25, €13.40) for adults, with concessions from students and seniors. There is a café and shop selling high quality products.

Should you go there in the morning, lunch in the **Union Hotel** opposite to the Fjord Centre is a great way of spending another hour. The restaurant serves high quality food with stunning views of the fjord and in your author's view, serves the best chips (French Fries) in the world! Have them with mayonnaise for pure perfection!

For younger, fitter and more agile cruise passengers with a yen for hiking, one of the best ways of spending your day would be to continue walking up the road, breathing air that is so fresh and clean that it almost hurts your nostrils, past gushing rivers and along a road lined with wild flowers from which you can gaze down on wooden farm buildings with grass  roofs (sometime being grazed by goats!).

Eventually you will arrive at the **Hotel The View (Hotel Utsikten)** which arguably affords the best view of them all. Kaiser Wilhelm thought so, anyway, and stayed in the hotel. Here.

This is not the highest viewpoint. That privilege is to be found from the mountain peak called *Dalsnibba,* well above the snowline. This view of the fjord and magnificent mountain backdrop is more expansive and breathtakingly beautiful.

A little further up the road is ***Flydalsjuvet Rock***, which is not unlike the Pulpit Rock in Hardanger fjord further south. Needless to say, this yet another impressive view of the fjord – but the most iconic images are of the rock itself, jutting out from the cliff edge and acting as a magnet for the brave (or insane, whichever way you look at it) who like to sit or stand on the very edge.

Equally hair-raising is a ship's excursion or bus trip from the Union Hotel in Geiranger or Geiranger itself to *Trollstigen (The Troll's Road)* and **Åndalsnes**.

The journey, which costs NOK 491 (£36.50, $48.15, €42.21 one-way!) begins with the bus climbing the 11 hairpin bends of the Eagle's Highway.

Following an old pack horse track, the 60-mile (100-kilometre) route, known as 'The Golden Route' or 'Route 63'. This takes you across the Trollstigeveien Plateau through the high valleys, past lakes, rushing rivers and rocky, snowy mountains.

You then descend to cross Tafjord to Valldalen – and then climb to the high mountain passes again until you reach Trollstigen.

Like the Eagle's Highway, there are 11 hairpin bends, but here, as the Visit Norway website puts it, is 'where you can feel the view hit you in your stomach. On this road, even the bravest can feel the adrenaline pump through their veins'.

In other words, if you don't have a head for heights, it is terrifying – and dangerous!

The road has a nine percent incline, is very narrow with barely enough passing room in places and is often subjected to rain and fog, which makes traction slippery. Despite this, it is one of the most visited attractions in Norway.

Snaking down to fjord level from its highest point at 2,814 feet (858 metres), the road took eight years to build (between 1916 and 1924) and is a remarkable feat of engineering.

As with the Flåm railway, you can't help wondering how they did it, but Norwegians are great mountaineers and engineers, and what they did was to give us some of the most gut-wrenchingly fabulous views on the planet.

If you have the nerve and want to do something else in Geiranger, take heart – you can do the same trip in reverse from our next port of call, Åndalsnes.

Setting sail from Geiranger is always a moment of excitement. That's because in most cases, cruise ships arrive early in the morning, so many people miss the sail-in. On the sailaway, it is easier to see the clifftop farms which harbour so many fantastic stories.

The Cruise Passenger's Guide to the Fjord People of Geiranger available at www.samhallbooks.com and Amazon.com.

***

ÅNDALSNES

Tourist companies like to call Åndalsnes *(pronounced 'awn' as in dawn)* the 'Mountaineering Capital' of Norway and with good reason; the town is encircled by the Romsdal mountains, often called the Norwegian Alps.

Strolling around and just out of town gives you the feeling of being somewhat insignificant, dwarfed as you are by the magnificent scenery.

It is one of those places where that awful word 'awesome' comes back into play.

Lying at the mouth of the River Rauma, close to the end of Romsdalsfjord, the town first became of interest to tourists in the late 19th century, when

English fly fishermen came to fish the salmon, now only just recovering after an infestation of a parasite in the 1980s.

It's not a big town. There are only 2,244 people living here at the last count. Nor is it overly rich in tourist attractions, but in terms of scenery there are few places to touch it.

Not surprisingly, the people of the town are immensely proud of their newest attraction, *The Norwegian Mountaineering Centre, (Norsk Tindesenter), which* opened in 2016.

It has to be said that the building itself is in modern parlance, somewhat 'in your face', dominating as it does

the harbour and views of the town and its mountain backdrop.

That said, the centre has quickly become renowned for containing Norway's highest indoor climbing wall, which remarkably, according to the website 'blurb', has climbing routes 'for everyone between the ages of three and 103 years'.

The wall has 60 different climbing routes with graded difficulty spread on 20 bolted holds. The great wall, known as Storveggen, is 21 metres (69 feet) high with 'a light overhang'.

Although cruise passengers tend to be of, or approaching, a certain age, this is a great place to visit and spend an hour learning about the people who climb mountains and the area itself.

The museum has descriptive information posts in both Norwegian and English, there is a 3D multimedia show to watch on a screen that simulates a rock wall, There are 16 different installations highlighting everything there is to know about mountaineering, as well as interactive entertainments, a café, a gift shop and a restaurant offering mountain pizza with reindeer meat.

Tickets cost NOK 145 (£12.90, $17, €14.90). The museum is open from 9am until 6pm year-round.

Having climbed the wall (?), you will now be ready for the main attraction that Åndalsnes has to offer: ***Troll Eggen (The Troll's Wall)***, a short taxi ride from the town centre.

If you thought Trollstigen *(The Troll's Highway)* was nerve-racking, the mere thought of climbing Trollsveggen is terrifying!

The wall itself is 5,577 ft (1,700 metres) high. The rock face is the highest vertical rock face in Europe, or 3,608 ft (1,100 metres) high with an overhang of nearly 165 ft (50 metres.

Yet, each year some of the world's most experienced mountaineers attempt the climb, which is rated extreme. This petrifying rock face also attracted base jumpers – people who jump off the sides of mountains with a parachute.

In the 1980s, more than 400 base jumpers launched themselves off the wall and, inevitably there were serious accidents, extremely risky and expensive rescue attempts, and fatalities.

In the end, the Norwegian authorities said enough was enough and in 1986 passed a law-making base jumping here illegal.

This was not without reason; as a memorial testifies, ten climbers and nine base jumpers lost their lives here.

The Trollveggen Visitor's Centre is locating just below the wall. Here you can see a film depicting the dramatic history of the wall and view the wall from its panoramic windows. There is a souvenir shop and café, too.

You can buy round trip tours locally to both Trollstigen and Trollveggen, with a 25-30 minute stop at both. Tickets cost of NOK 550 (£49, $65, €56.50), which given that this is Norway is a very reasonable price for a good day's outing.

Alternatively, you may prefer a gentler, less vertiginous way to see the mountain scenery and take the Rauma train, which leaves from the station right next to your ship's berth.

Incidentally, the *Åndalsnes Tourist Centre* is in the same building as the station – a cosy place with a small café and lots of information and helpful people.

The Tourist Information office is in the grey station building at the right foreground of the picture.

The Rauma Railway is a dedicated sightseeing train running four times a day from May to August. It is a wonderful opportunity to experience the countryside between Åndalsnes and Dombås, a journey of approximately one hour and 40 minutes. Round trip tickets cost NOK 600 (£53.54, $70.40, €61.70), which again is reasonable given that the return journey takes three hours.

Incidentally, parts of the *Harry Potter and the Half-Blood Prince* were shot alongside the Rauma Railway

The coaches are air conditioned with a toilet and wheelchair elevator. The route rises to 2,150 ft (655 metres) and passes over 32 bridges, through six tunnels, one of them nearly a mile long.

There is a running commentary and passengers are given a map and booklet about the journey. Importantly, the train slows down at all the main viewpoints.

On your return to Åndalsnes, be sure to visit the only *Chapel Train* in Norway and possibly in the world. You will find it just outside the station close to your ship.

The Norwegian State Railway gave the carriage to the Church of Norway when they retired it for a newer version.

The carriage was consecrated by the Bishop Bondevik in June 2003, a service attended by King Harald and Queen Sonja.

The carriage still has the original seating but with an altar and small font. It is tended by the Church of Norway, the Salvation Army and the Pentecostal Church.

From the train chapel to the Cruise Terminal is a mere few yards. Lunch anybody?

***

MOLDE, ATLANTIC HIGHWAY, HÅHOLMEN & BUD

One of the challenges when writing about a cruise up the coast of Norway is to find a different form for the phrase 'one of the most beautiful'.

No matter which port you arrive at, almost all of them have a backdrop of mountains and a foreground of fjords, islands, skerries or the Atlantic Ocean.

Whether you are in Bergen, Florø, Ålesund, Tromsø or Alta, or most places south, north or in between, you will happily be able to talk about snow-capped mountains and stunning scenery.

Molde, on the northern shore of the Romsdalsfjord seaward of Åndalsnes, is no different, facing as it does almost the entire range of the Romsdal mountain range and a plethora of islands and islets.

Almost every house in this city of 25,000 people has a fabulous view. Nicknamed the 'City of Roses', Molde has a rich history. It began life as a minor trading port in the early 15th century and gradually evolved into a town reliant on timber and herring exports.

In the mid-1600s, following the defeat of Denmark (of which Norway was a part) by Sweden during the so-called Northern wars, Molde also became a focal point for a Resistance movement against the Swedes.

Centuries later, Molde had evolved into a prosperous commercial centre for the Romsdal region, earning its keep from textiles, clothing and eventually tourism.

Kaiser Wilhelm often came here in the summer, as did the Prince of Wales, attracted by luxury hotels surrounded by picturesque wooden houses, attractive squares, parks and gardens blooming with roses.

Not for nothing did Molde become known as 'The City of Roses'. It still is, with the city blooming with fragrant roses from June until the end of August each year, the largest planting of them being on the Town Hall roof.

A major fire in in January 1916 destroyed one-third of the city. The cause was never discovered although arson seems the most likely, given that a Molde judge convicted a man of arson a few weeks earlier and banished him from the city.

During the Second World War, in April and May 1940, German bombers destroyed more than two-thirds of the city.

By then, King Haakon and the Crown Prince, Olav, had fled Oslo and, after a dramatic flight lasting some two months, eventually reached relative safety on the outskirts of Molde.

They were followed by members of the government and the country's gold reserve, which was hidden in a textile factory.

When the Germans discovered the whereabouts of the refugees, they intensified the air raids, which destroyed the old wooden church and left the city in a sea of flames.

True to their tradition, many people in Molde belonged to the Resistance and with their help, the royals and the government were able to escape on a British warship, HMS Glasgow, to England, where they set up a government in exile.

After the war, Molde expanded exponentially and is today not only an administrative centre for the Romsdal region but also one of its most industrious towns, widely diversified with farming and fishing, commerce, tourism, and industry, notably producing thrusters for ocean going ships.

Molde is also the annual venue for an internationally famous jazz festival.

One of the city's main attractions is the **Romsdal Museum,** originally created in 1912 and just a short walk out of the downtown area.

The museum comprises a new exhibition centre inaugurated in 2016 and one of the largest collections of old buildings from different parts of Norway now set in an attractive park complete with duck pond and plenty of benches and picnic areas.

There are several exhibitions in the museum centre, as well as a café, shop, library and a display area where you can see the process of making what we call the 'national' costume, known as a *'bunad'* in Norwegian. In fact, the *bunad* is not national at all and actually differs from one region to another, and often from one valley to another.

The museum park is every day open year-round from 8 am until 10 pm and there is no entry charge. The Museum Centre charges NOK 100 (£8.95, $11.75, €10.30) with a NOK 20 (£1.80, $2.35, €2.05) discount for seniors and students.

Outside Molde, the greatest attraction is the ***Atlantic Highway***, which was constructed by building eight bridges over a series of islands and skerries spanning some 5.2 miles (8.3 kilometres.

This region is known as the ***Hustadvika*** coast, renowned for its beauty and terrible storms, which often result in the road being flooded and cars drenched by massive waves.

As fascinating in summer as it is dramatic during a storm.

One of the best ways to see the Atlantic Highway and the lovely rolling farmland inland is to take a round trip from Molde bus terminal. This costs NOK 305 (£28.00, $36.00, €32) per person and is well worth it for the experience.

Passengers are given the opportunity to walk on a suspended walkway around the islet of Eldhusø (*lit:* Fire House island), where there is a café and toilets.

Just over half a mile (one kilometre) off the Atlantic Highway is Håholmen (*pron: haw-holmen),* was once a small island community comprising 25 cottages for fishermen and pilots, and their workplaces, harbour and wharfs dating back to the 1700s.

Ragnar Thorseth, the first Norwegian to achieve the North Pole (with Trygve Berge), inherited the island which his grandfather, a pilot for the fishing captains who lived there, bought in 1898.

Thorseth's father, who owned the island before him, was a pilot for the fishermen. The seaward side of the island faces directly onto the Atlantic and in summer affords fabulous sunsets which turn the coast into a glow of golden light reminiscent of the old Benson & Hedges advertisements and commercials.

It was here that Thorseth reconstructed his Viking ship Saga *Siglar*, which ultimately sank in a hurricane off Valencia, Spain after circumnavigating the globe.

In 1960, Håholmen ceased to be a centre for fishing and Thorseth eventually sold it. Today, it is run as a hotel and conference centre by the Norwegian company, Classic Norway. The cottages have all been refurbished, but retain the original character. They all have superb views of the island and the ocean.

There is also an excellent restaurant and if you happen to have a long piece of string, clothes peg and a stone, and lean over the edge of the jetty, you will very likely land a crab or a lobster. The chefs will cook them for you in minutes – the freshest seafood that you will ever taste.

The island also boasts a small museum containing the remains of Saga Siglar and you can sit in a Viking ship to watch the film of Thorseth's exploits.

Access to the island from the Atlantic Highway is either by motor boat or a ten-minute ride on a replica of Saga *Siglar,* which was itself the most authentic replica of a Viking ocean going trading ship, known as a *knarr.*

At the western end of the Atlantic Highway is **Bud** *(pron: Bewd as in lewd),* a 16th-17th century fishing village, which once was the largest trading port on this part of the west coast.

The village has a population of just 760 people and several good fish restaurants.

During the Second World War, Hitler was convinced that the allied forces would invade Norway (and Churchill was happy to keep him thinking that; Britain even invented a fake army to sustain the myth). As a result, German troops built many concrete fortifications at Bud and along the Hustadvika coast.

The coastal fort at Bud is today a war memorial and museum, which stages exhibitions depicting events from the war. There are also some excellent views of the village and the Hustavika coast here.

The best way to get to Bud is to take the 532 or 533 bus, which leaves hourly from Molde Bus Station *(Molde Trafikterminal).* The journey takes approximately one hour and 20 minutes, including a 25-

minute stop at Einesvågen school. The cost is NOK 239 (£21.50, $28.15, €24.63) for the round trip. You can book tickets at this link:

https://www.visitnorway.com/places-to-go/fjord-norway/northwest/listings-northwest/roundtrip-by-bus-molde-bud-molde/193044/

***

TRONDHEIM

Located at the junction of the River Nidelva and Trondheim fjord, Trondheim is Norway's third largest city, with a population of 193,501, some 40,000 of whom are students who play no small part in making this a charming, vibrant place to visit.

It is charming because the River Nidelva, lined with old wooden warehouses, flows through the city centre and vibrant because its pedestrian streets brim over with shoppers, student buskers and street theatre performers.

There are countless restaurants and bars serving locally brewed beers. There is an 11th century cathedral with a magnificent façade and Archbishop's Palace and this city of learning has an impressive history and plenty of sites to see.

Rock carvings from the region prove that people lived here for thousands of years but the city's history really begins in Viking times.

Harald Fairhair (865-933 AD) was proclaimed king here, as was his son, Haakon the Good, but it was Olaf Tryggvasson (his name is also spelt Olav) who is credited not only with founding the city in 997, but also bringing Christianity to the Viking World and the Northern regions, including Iceland and Greenland.

His statue perched on top of an obelisk dominates the main square and his name crops up in one form or another just about everywhere.

The plinth also functions as a sundial, which is only accurate in the winter months because it doesn't allow for the change to summer time.

In 997, King Olaf, who was later afforded a sainthood, named the town Kaupangen, which meant 'the market place'. As an important trading post, it was the capital of Norway from then until 1217.

In 1152, the city became the seat of the Catholic Archdiocese of Nidaros, and Kaupangen assumed the name Nidaros for some 400 years, until 1537.

The name changed several times after that. During the Norwegian-Danish Union, it became Trondhjem *(pronounced Trond-yem)*, but officials later decided to revert to the name Nidaros because they wanted to retain a link to the city's historic past.

That didn't go down at all well. In 1928, the authorities held a referendum as to which name to keep; a massive 91% majority voted for the current Trondheim.

However, two years later, the authorities decided for reasons best known to themselves to re-introduce Nidaros as the official name, anyway, a decision which provoked outrage.

Rioting erupted on the streets and became so intense that the Storting (parliament) relented and the city finally became known as Trondheim.

During the Second World War, the Germans tried to change the name to Drontheim, but this faded into obscurity at the end of the war.

In medieval times, Trondheim was almost entirely comprised of wooden buildings and whilst fires were fairly common in all cities and towns at the time, Trondheim seemed especially susceptible.

Huge fires swept through the city at least nine times, especially in 1651, when 90% of it was destroyed, and again 30 years later when the entire town had to be rebuilt.

This time, the city planners called for wide boulevards that could serve as fire breaks. They still do, but just as importantly they lend to the city a sense of dignity and pride.

During the Second World War, Trondheim received particularly harsh treatment from the Germans, who imposed martial law following various acts of sabotage by the Norwegian Resistance, including the shooting of two German police officers.

It is thought that this enraged the Head of the Occupation Forces in Norway, Josef Terboven, (see *The Resistance: Norway's Paper Clip War'* on page 75) to such an extent that he declared martial law on Trondheim, as well as throughout the entire counties of Nord-Trøndelag and Grane, and more than a dozen other municipalities.

During this time, Terboven authorised the executions of 10 leading Norwegians, including a lawyer, a newspaper editor, the president of a bank and a theatre director. They were described as *'soneofre'* *(lit: zone offerings)*. Whatever the name, they were sacrificial lambs murdered without any kind of trial or legal process for no other reason than payback.

Shortly afterwards, Terboven reinforced his iron fist reputation by ordering the murders of another 24 individuals who were taken into a forest, bound and blindfolded, and shot two at a time in front of an open grave. Their crime? They were deemed hostile to the German state., which is hardly surprising given the occupation!

Martial law lasted six days, during which time a 5pm-9am curfew was enforced. Nobody was allowed to travel by train or long distances. Tobacco sales were banned and nearly 100 other individuals are arrested.

The Germans harboured hopes of transforming Trondheim into its principal naval base and did build a major submarine base there, but failed to make it a base.

Fifteen miles northeast of Trondheim and 60 miles inland, the German battleship *Tirpitz* lay in Faettenfjord, poised to dart out at any time to attack the Atlantic convoys carrying guns, planes, ammunition and other valuable cargoes to Murmansk in Russia.

The ship was protected by multiple anti-aircraft batteries ashore, double anti-submarine nets, underwater listening probes, hydrophones and smoke generators in the surrounding mountains. These would generate a smokescreen to try to hide *Tirpitz* from any overhead aircraft.

The British Royal Air Force carried out several bombing raids on the ship, all of them unsuccessful. *Tirpitz* was later moved to Tromsø, where she was later discovered and sunk by a single Tallboy bomb dropped from 10,000 feet and travelling at the speed of sound.

After the war, Trondheim gradually became a great centre of education and learning, so much so that today one-fifth of the population (42,000) are students.

The Norwegian University of Science and Technology is the largest in Norway with an international focus and nine faculties of engineering, information technology and electrical engineering, natural sciences, architecture and design, economics and management, medicine and health sciences, social and educational sciences, humanities and a museum.

Cooperating closely with the University of Science and Technology (NTNU), St. Olaf's is a teaching hospital and a regional hospital for Central Norway.

Trondheim also boasts three of the largest independent research institutions in Scandinavia with 1,800 employees, 1,300 in Trondheim. The Geological Survey of Norway is located at Lade in Trondheim and is a major geoscientific institution with 220 employees of which 70% are scientists.

There are also 11 high schools in the city. Trondheim Cathedral School was founded in 1152 and is the oldest upper secondary school (gymnasium) in Norway.

Not surprisingly, students have influenced the culture in Trondheim significantly. Well over 1,000 volunteers run the student society. Students organise two major culture festivals and the University lists more than 200 different student organisations with web pages on its servers.

The University's music conservatory, renowned as one of the most innovative in the world, has created strong support and interest in jazz and classical music, with rock music not far behind. The city has both a symphony and a jazz orchestra and hosts an annual jazz festival. The national museum of popular music, Rockheim, is dedicated collecting, preserving and sharing Norwegian popular music from the 1950s to the present day.

From the port, shuttle buses take passengers to a side street a stone's throw from *Nidaros Cathedral*, an impressive church built over the grave of St. Olav, and the Archbishop's Palace adjacent to it.

Construction began in 1070 but it took nearly 150 years before it was finished, having taken on elements of both Gothic and Romanesque architecture.

No sooner was it built than it became the most important site for Christian pilgrims with the faithful arriving from as far afield as Oslo and central and southern Sweden.

Known as St. Olaf's way, the main route was a trek of some 650 kilometres (about 400 miles), and for anybody who has the time and the will to attempt it, *The Pilgrim Centre* in Trondheim provides advice and serves as a meeting place and reception centre for all pilgrims who complete the journey – and even those who don't or just turn up with 'the mind of a pilgrim'. Certificates are awarded to pilgrims who complete the journey.

It is also a hostel and a retreat offering workshops and seminars on themes related to the theology of pilgrimage, the heritage of Saint Olaf and inter-religious dialogue.

You can contact them at post@dpilegrimsgarden.no or +47 73 52 50 00. There is also a Pilgrim's Office in Oslo at Akersbakken 30, 0172 Oslo. Email: oslo@pilegrim.info, Tel +47 480 52 949).

The Cathedral, with its dual bell towers and intricate façade, replete with arches, windows and pillars, is one of the largest medieval cathedrals in Scandinavia.

A succession of Norwegian kings were crowned in the Cathedral during the Middle Ages, but the practice ended with the coronation of King Haakon VII in 1906. After that Kings and Queens were consecrated rather than crowned, beginning with King Olav V in 1957.

King Harald V and Queen Sonja, were consecrated there in 1991.

Nidaros Cathedral is open from 9am to 2pm Monday to Saturday and from 1pm to 4pm on Sundays. Entrance costs NOK 100 (£9.00, $11.85, €10.35) with no concession for seniors.

Adjacent to the Cathedral is the *Archbishop's Palace Museum*, which houses medieval artefacts from what was the Archbishop's palace prior to the reformation, including the Archbishop's mint where coins were stamped. Three mints, stacked one on top of the other, are said to be the smallest and northernmost in the world, but in this part of the world almost everything claims to be 'the most northerly', not always with justification!

Excavation of the grounds in the 1990s by more than 100 archaeologists, many from abroad, produced about 160,000 artefacts and the foundations of about 100 buildings.

The Palace museum also has on display more than 100 medieval sculptures, several of them original sculptures from the Cathedral's west façade. There are also models of what the Archbishop's Palace complex looked like at different stages of its history.

Entry times Tuesday-Friday between 11 am and 2pm, 11am -3pm on Saturdays and 12-4pm on Sundays. Entrance fees are the same as for the Cathedral. Walking to the eastern end of the Cathedral and then along Bispegata or through the church gardens to the river, you come to the *Old Town Bridge (Gamle Bybro)*.

The first wooden bridge, supported by stone piers, was built in 1681 as part of the town's reconstruction following the disastrous fire of that year. It was completed four years later with an iron gate at the centre.

The bridge served as a guarded entry and exit point with strategic military importance until 1816. A guardhouse and excise house at the western (Cathedral) end of the bridge is today a nursery school.

The bridge has undergone many repairs and alterations but the orange painted iron portal remains. It is still known as the Portal of Happiness (*Lykkens Portal*) after a song written by a composer later executed in 1943 on Terboven's orders as an 'atonement sacrifice'. Thankfully, Terboven blew himself up at the end of the war!

Just beyond the bridge on the eastern bank of the river is the ***Trampe Bicycle Lift***, ***(Sykkelheis)*** and now known as the CycloCable. This is the first and some say only bicycle escalator in the world.

Opened in 1993 to enable cyclists to ride up the steep hill easily and avoid arriving for work exhausted and perspiring, the lift was built with the stated aim of persuading more people to ride bicycles instead of driving cars.

Cyclists merely place one foot on the lifts angled platform and the lift pushes them automatically up the hill at a speed of around five miles an hour.

So far, it has carried a quarter of a million cyclists up the 492 ft (150 metre) hill but its great advantage is that it can transport anybody with a small-wheeled vehicle from mothers with a pram to a child on a scooter.

The lift takes cyclists from the river almost to the *Kristiansten Fortress (Krianstenfestning)*, which was also built after the great fire of 1681.

Affording excellent views over the city, the fortress enabled Norwegian troops to repel Swedish attackers in 1718, thus saving Trondheim from the indignity of being conquered.

The fort was also used by the Nazis during the Second World War and was the site on which 23 Norwegian patriots were executed.

Complete with dungeon and museum, and surrounded by parkland, the fort has become one of Trondheim's main attractions.

The Norwegian flag is raised whenever the fort is open, which is between 9 am and 6 pm every day during the summer. Entrance is free.

Back on the river bank, old wooden warehouses stand like sentinels along the natural harbour.

For centuries, they were used for storing cargoes from ships entering the river. Each property comprised a

narrow alleyway running from the river front inland.

These were lined with wooden buildings, which inevitably were vulnerable to fire. Happily, they were always restored to their original state and today they are used mostly for offices, apartments, restaurants and shops.

Cross back over the Old Town Bridge and turn right, then left into Vår Frue Strete or Kongens gate, and you will come to the main square and marketplace.

Turn right again along Munkegata and you arrive in the buzzing shopping area, a favourite venue for buskers and street performers.

Colourful shopping area, central Trondheim.

If Trondheim is renowned as a city of students and education, it is no less known for the multitude of museums.

These range from the Museums of Arts, Decorative Arts, Japanese arts and crafts, Science, Natural History and Archaeology to the Maritime museum, the Music and Musical Instrument museum, Tramway museum, Jewish museum and not least Rockheim, the National Discovery Centre for Pop and Rock music.

Back at the port, you will see a small island called **Munkholmen (Monk's Island).** The Trondheim City website notes that during Viking times, this popular tourist attraction was where the Vikings held public executions. It was also where Olaf Tryggvason put his enemies' heads on poles after battling for kingdom and Christianity in 995 AD.

The island used to be called Nidarholm, which means 'River Nid islet' but the name was changed after a Benedictine monastery as built there.

Later, Munkholmen was used as a prison and then as a fort by the Germans during the occupation.

The island is now a recreation area with a small beach, a café, and a restaurant which opens every Wednesday between 27th June and 8th August. A boat service runs during the day between May and September, departing from Ravnkloa. Tickets cost about NOK 5 less than the Cathedral entrance fee.

So, despite the wealth of ways to spend your time in Trondheim, I do recall a cruise passenger returning to the ship mid-morning and saying: "It's a one-horse town. There's nothing worth seeing apart from the Cathedral."

As people say in the north of England: "There's nowt so strange as folk!"

***

BRONNØSUND

Some cruise passengers wonder why on earth their ship has called in at Brønnøysund because there is not a lot to do there. The centre is modern but not particularly interesting and there are few excursions available.

The answer, of course, is that it is yet another picturesque little town in the midst of wonderful coastal scenery.

Road signs refer to it as 'the coastal town in the middle of Norway' because it is equidistant to the North Cape and to Lindesnes, Norway's southernmost land point.

With a population of approximately 4,700 inhabitants, the town is surprisingly prosperous. It was here that *Fjord Seafood,* a highly successful local fish processing company was founded in 1992.

The largest limestone mine in northern Europe is also located here, producing limestone ingredients for a multitude of products from cement to toothpaste and paint, and the town is said to produce more foodstuffs than anywhere else in northern Norway.

Brønnøysund's modern town centre. Below: view from a local restaurant

Other industries centred here include agriculture, hydroponics, wood processing and transport – not to mention all important tourism. It is also the base for Torghattan ASA, a shipping company, which operates bus and car and passenger ferries, travel agencies, real estate and security.

So Brønnøysund has more going for it than first impressions might suggest.

Despite the small population, Brønnøysund has an airport and a direct connection to the main E6 highway.

The town's chief claim to fame, however, is its proximity to **_Torghatten_**, its legendary granite mountain, which means 'square hat' and has a hole right through it.

A Nordland fairy tale of trolls that froze to stone and became mountains along the coast has it that the 258-metre (846 foot) mountain is the ancient troll King of Brønnøy's hat.

Early one morning, the king, known as The Horseman, saw a beautiful maiden called Lekamøya and her seven virgin sisters bathing in the sea. The Horseman was immediately consumed with love for her and decided there and then to kidnap her at midnight.

As he galloped towards them, his cape flaring behind him, a rival troll king, Vågekallen, who desperately needed a wife, watched from a mountain nearby.

Lekamøya and her sisters ran until they could run no further. The Horseman fired an arrow towards them but just in time, Vågekallen threw his hat towards the maidens to protect them.

By good fortune, the arrow pierced the hat but at that very moment, the sun appeared and its rays turned the trolls, the hat, and all of them into stone.

Believe that and you will believe anything!

In fact, geologists have confirmed that the hole, which is 160 metres long, 30 metres high and 25 metres wide (525 ft x 98.4 ft x 82ft), was caused by the erosion of ice.

Another suggestion is that as the tectonic plates collided, the mountain was pushed upwards after the sea had eroded the hole in the rock. Whichever version you prefer, it definitely wasn't caused by trolls!

You can drive and cycle easily to Torghatten and walk to the top and into the hole – which affords stupendous views of the coast and its islands.

For the historically minded, ***Skarsåsen Fortress*** is located about 5 km or 3 miles on the outskirts of Brønnøysund city centre.

Built by the Nazis, who ran an internment camp for Russian prisoners nearby during the Second World War, it comprises bunkers, four 15.5 cm guns with a range of 17,000 metres (55,774 ft), emplacements with adjoining trenches, many defence positions and the remnants of the German barracks, which housed 120 men.

This meant the battery was undermanned compared with the normal complement of 235 men.

In some of the tunnels they dug, there is a small risk of landslides, should you decide to visit the fortress.

As I mentioned at the beginning of this article, Brønnøysund is not rich in sightseeing venues rather than a great port for enjoying the coastal and mountain scenery for very little expense.

So, as cruise staff will always tell you: "Whatever you do, enjoy your day!"

***

LOFOTEN

Leknes-Gravdal, Ballstad, Flakstad & Nusfjord

The Lofoten Wall

It is often said that the voyage north along the west coast of Norway is the most beautiful in the world and to that, I would add only that arguably the most beautiful section of that voyage is the Lofoten *(pron: Lu-futn)* Islands.

Although they are a chain of islands some 62 miles (100 kms) long, Norwegians always refer to them simply as 'Lofoten'.

Depending on the size of your ship and the route it is taking, you will either travel approximately 15 miles (24 kms) to the west of the spectacular mountain range known as the Lofoten Wall or, if you are lucky, up the great Vestfjord, calling in at one or more of Lofoten's ports.

The difficulty with Lofoten is that you can throw superlatives at them until kingdom come and still get nowhere near touching the reality of their staggering beauty.

Spectacular, awesome, incomparable, unparalleled, fabulous, outstanding, dramatic - these are all true, but they come nowhere close to describing the feeling in your gut when you first arrive there. Suffice to say they comprise 475 square miles (1,227 sq. kms) of grandeur.

No matter whether it is summer or winter, Lofoten is a photographer's paradise. Indeed, in winter, when the mountains are blanketed with snow, they are even more stunning.

Everywhere you go, you will be dwarfed by high, craggy, mountains towering as high as 3,300 ft (1,000 metres) above the brightly coloured fishing villages and their wooden huts known as *rørbuer (pron: Rur – as in fur – boo-er)*, huddled together in rows of vibrant reds and yellows.

Hardly surprising, then, that Lofoten attracts more than one million tourists each year.

On rocky outcrops, racks of timber await the drying season for the muscular, teenage cod known as *skrei (pron: skray)* that spawn offshore from January to March.

These fish are the lifeblood of Lofoten, for whose people the motto is 'In Cod We Trust'. The ocean, they say, is 'our larder and our well-being'.

Top chefs around the world agree that these cod are the tastiest in the world, best steamed to preserve the brilliant whiteness and served simply with boiled potatoes and a very light (ideally champagne sauce).

But top chefs are not the only ones who appreciate the abundance of fish; Otters also think it is paradise! Indeed, Lofoten has more sea eagles, cormorants, puffins and other seabirds than anywhere else in Europe.

The chain of islands lies almost 100 miles (160 kms) north of the Arctic Circle and are said to resemble the shape of a lynx's foot.

People have lived on the islands for at least 11,000 years and first introduced agriculture and livestock around 250 BC.

We tend to think of the Vikings living only in the west and southwestern parts of Norway, but they settled here in the early Viking age and probably began the cod fisheries roughly 1,000 years ago.

Lofoten is also blessed with the midnight sun, the other side of that coin being the harsh, dark winters.

Life for the population was hard and many were the times when poverty and near starvation were the norm.

One old man tried to make a living selling pocket watches, rowing between the mainland across the Vestfjord from Bodø and back, with the watches nestling in numerous pockets sown into his overcoat. It was a journey of nearly 70 miles and took a couple of days each way, by which time his coat glistened with frost and frozen sea spray.

Today, he could have driven along the main E10 route connecting Lofoten to the mainland. This section of the road opened officially in 2007. It means that instead of a four or five-hour journey including a ferry trip, the bus from Svolvaer to Harstad and Narvik airport now takes only three hours, including several stops.

Today, all the main islands are connected by bridges or tunnels, one of which is more than 4.2 miles (six kilometres) long.

Leknes-Gravdal

Cruise ships berth midway between these two communities. Leknes, a short shuttle bus ride away, is a functional community often used as a refuelling and provisioning stop for tourists driving the E10 route, a journey that can take as long as four days!

The town, which lies at the centre of Lofoten and is home to 3,176 inhabitants, is the largest in the Vestvågøy district, which in turn has a population of approximately 11,000 people.

The ship's berth is about four kilometres (3½ miles) from the town, which is one of the few towns in Lofoten that are not located by the sea. As a consequence, you will not find the traditional wooden *røbuer* here.

Indeed, many cruise passengers find the town rather boring because it is geared primarily as the main retail centre.

Other tourists say it is a welcome relief from the almost overpowering grandeur of the surrounding landscape.

If you Google 'Things to do in Leknes', you really won't find very much. There is a **Fisheries Museum**, which gives a comprehensive look at fishing boats, tackle, the process of splitting, salting and drying cod, and also reflects the myths, beliefs and superstitions of the fishermen of yore.

Sadly, there is not much else. Even the official Leknes websites suggest that the main attractions lie outside the town.

However, the village of **Gravdal,** which lies four kilometres southwest of Leknes, is a different story. You can take a taxi there from the ship's berth but make sure you arrange a pickup point and time for your return to the ship.

Otherwise, Gravdal is a one and a quarter mile (two-kilometre) walk from the ship's berth in the opposite direction to Leknes.

Although there is very little to see in Gravdal, the walk is a fabulous experience and the scenery is wonderful. Here, you can wander amongst fields of wild flowers in summer, meander round the rocky inlets and visit the imposing ***Buksnes Stave Church.***

Buksnes stave church, Gravdal

Gravdal is described as one of the larger villages in the region but, in fact, it has a population of only 1,663 and is what I would describe as a 'scattered village'. In other words, apart from a few odd houses and a main street with little other than trees and a bus stop, there's not a lot to it.

Wikipedia describes the population density as being 1,309 inhabitants per square kilometre (0.37 square miles). That means the chances of seeing anyone during your meanderings are extremely slim.

That, of course, is the beauty of Gravdal. You have the place more or less to yourself, not least because most cruise passengers head straight for Leknes 'because there's nothing to see in the opposite direction'. Wrong!

For anyone who appreciates countryside, seascapes and bird and wildlife, Gravdal and its environs are heaven.

Perhaps most remarkable is the clarity of the air. There is no dust or pollution so every breath you take in is sweet, as if you have never experienced anything quite like it before. Indeed, you probably haven't!

There is no litter. Not a scrap of paper anywhere, so everything is pristine. The sad aspect of all this is that you probably won't notice it until you are in the next city breathing vehicle fumes. Then, you will remember!

Most cruise lines offer excursions to the surrounding fjords and towns and one trip, in particular is worth the expense. That is a bus tour from Leknes to ***Ballstad, Flakstad and Nusfjord.***

Despite a population of only 826 people, ***Ballstad*** is said to be one of the largest fishing villages in Lofoten., which doesn't say a lot for the rest of them. It lies about three miles (5 kms) out of Leknes.

Fisherman's cottage with Ballstad and Skottinden in the distance

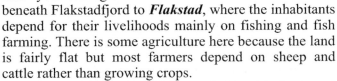

The village is dominated by the 2,201 ft (671-metre-high mountain **Skottinden,** which is notable because it has four summits, three slightly less high on its southern ridge.

From Ballstad, your bus will take you through the tunnel beneath Flakstadfjord to **Flakstad**, where the inhabitants depend for their livelihoods mainly on fishing and fish farming. There is some agriculture here because the land is fairly flat but most farmers depend on sheep and cattle rather than growing crops.

Flakstad Church, which was built with driftwood from Siberia, dates back to 1780. A chandelier and the altar table are also from Siberia.

A church has stood on the site since 1430 and possibly earlier. Unfortunately, a hurricane destroyed it in the mid-18th century.

Flakstad leaves you with a sense of isolation and tranquillity. No doubt, this is a harsh landscape in which to live during the winter months but in summer it is enervating.

From Flakstad, your tour bus will take you through rugged countryside, past a huge lake called Storvatten (*lit:* Big Water) and along a winding, twisting road on the bank of the narrow Nusfjord.

Nusfjord is everything you would expect of a costal village in Lofoten. It is one of the oldest and best preserved fishing villages, complete with drying racks for the cod ans surrounded by steep mountains.

Many of the rørbuar are now rented out to holidaymakers, some of whom describe their experiences ecstatically on the internet; 'takes you to that happy place within yourself' … 'a feeling of being truly alive' ... 'didn't want to leave' ... 'the kind of place a writer would go to finish the last chapter of their novel' ... and so on.

It says everything! What more could you want?

***

LOFOTEN

Stamsund, Svolvaer, Henningsvaer, Trollfjord

Stamsund, Lofoten

Stamsund is a charming coastal community of about 1,000 people, yet despite being sparsely populated it is the largest base for the Lofoten trawl fishery and is especially busy between December and April when the cod come to spawn.

Lying on the island of Vestvågøy's southern coast, it spans several islets and has numerous harbours.

The *Hurtigruten* ships call in twice a day with supplies, passengers and tourists, once northbound and once on the return southbound trip.

The community has taken great care to restore the colourful *rørbuer* to pristine condition and most of them today are available to rent as holiday homes.

The town economy relies primarily on tourism and fishing. Two of the trawling and processing companies in Stamsund are the largest in Norway, producing and exporting cod, haddock and pollock (also known as saithe or coley), and fish products.

The principal attractions for visitors are the midnight sun, hiking in the mountain scenery, boat and fishing trips, pristine white sand beaches in summer and the Northern Lights in winter.

Indeed, for all its small community, Stamsund has more to offer, not least the 90-seat ***Nordland Visual Theatre (Nordland Figurteateret)***.

Founded in 2001, the annual Stamsund International Theatre Festival comprises a week of performances and festivities designed to enhance the international exchange of performance arts.

The theatre offers all the technical, production and daily operation required by for a theatre performance, all under the same roof.

It also provides apartments for visiting actors and theatre workers and boasts a library with an open fireplace (!), a sewing room and puppet workshop.

Stamsund also has the distinction of being the scene of the first successful raid on German occupied territory.

High above the town on the 3,809 ft (1,161 metre) mountain, Higravstinden, a complex of bunkers and lookout points remind us of the occupation.

Here, during Operation Claymore, a force comprising Nos. 3 and 4 Commando, some 50 Royal Engineers and a group of Free Norwegian forces attacked the town and took 228 German troops prisoner.

They also returned with 314 loyal Norwegian volunteers, several Quisling collaborators and codebooks, and wheels for the Enigma machine, although they failed to find an actual Enigma machine as they had hoped.

Such was the success of the raid, however, that with typical British and Norwegian humour, a telegram was despatched to Adolf Hitler to let him know how useless the German forces had been.

Hitler responded by despatching an SS unit to oversee operations there.

Further up the coast, *Svolvaer* is the largest town and *de facto* capital of Lofoten with a population of some 5,000 people.

It is as modern as any town elsewhere in Norway with supermarkets, shopping malls, a multitude of shops, hotels and first-rate restaurants, and attractive art galleries open year-round.

What really appeals about Svolvaer, though, is that wherever you are, there is a photograph to be taken. The scenery is utterly ... well, here we go with the superlatives again, but every one of them justified!

As with Stamsund, the economy relies primarily on the fisheries industry.

Deep-sea fishing in the fjords is also popular with tourists and professional fishermen. For two days in March each year, Svolvaer plays host to the World Cod Fishing Championships, which regularly attract more than 600 passionate anglers from abroad, all hoping to land a 66lb (30 kilo) fish.

They fish from 9am until 2pm, then head back to

port where as many as 6,000 spectators turn out to watch the fish being weighed. There are two categories: Prizes for the largest fish and for the largest number of fish.

On the Friday, it doesn't matter what kind of fish you land – cod, wolf-fish, halibut, you name it – they all count. Cod fishing, especially fishing for Skrei, goes back 1,000 years and has been a major factor in the history and culture of Lofoten through the centuries.

The 490-foot (150-metre) granite mountain, *Svolvaergeita,* which affords on of the most popular climbing routes in Norway, dominates Svolvaer.

At the summit are two towers with a five-foot (one and a half metre) gap between them, a magnet for climbers who feel the need to jump from one to the other.

It is said – and I have no wish to prove the claim – that when you do jump the gap, you can see the town's graveyard below.

Technically, the climb is said to be fairly easy, but it is extremely steep so you would need a good head for heights and rock-climbing experience, for the route is not to be tackled without ropes and proper climbing equipment.

For those who like to observe mountains from ground level, an alternative to climbing Svolvaergeita might be to visit the *Lofoten War Museum (Lofoten Kringsminnemuseum-Museum Nord*, located at Fiskergata No. 3.

Certainly, one of the best war museums in Norway, the Lofoten War Museum houses an impressive display of uniforms and artefacts from the occupation years. These include a watercolour landscape painting and several coloured drawings of Snow White and the Seven Dwarves – by Adolf Hitler.

The museum also tells the story in photographs of the British commando raid on Austvågøy, during which they torched (with the help of the local population) oil storage tanks, herring oil plants and a huge factory ship used to produce nearly 200 tons of fish a day.

The Germans retaliated by burning homes and farms and taking 64 hostages who spent the rest of the war in a prison camp.

The museum's collection comprises 140 uniforms, a gallery of photographs and a plethora of fascinating odds and ends. These include Christmas decorations covered with swastikas and a visiting card holder belonging to Eva Braun, Hitler's mistress.

The museum is an excellent way of spending a couple of hours and regularly receives extremely positive feedback from all over the world.

It is open daily between 10 am and 4pm Monday to Friday and 11am to 3pm at weekends between June 1 and September 30. Otherwise, it is open daily between 6.30pm and 10pm except for Christmas Eve. Entrance fee is NOK 100 (£9.05, $11.80, €10.35) with no concessions for seniors.

Then there is the *North Norwegian Art Centre* located in the town square (Torget 20), which annually curates half a dozen or more changing exhibitions of contemporary art and crafts by Norwegian and international artists.

Many of the artworks displayed are also for sale in the museum shop.

The Centre is open Tuesday to Sunday from 10am until 3pm (Closed Mondays). There is no entry charge.

On the quayside is another unique attraction – a Magic Ice Bar. As the name suggests, this is a permanent exhibition constructed entirely of crystal clear ice.

Although there are several ice bars in Norway and elsewhere, the Svolvaer bar claims to be one of the largest in the world and displays numerous ice sculptures.

Visitors are provided with warm clothing 'to cover you from head to ankle, including gloves' and are given a free welcome drink served, as you would expect, in a glass made from ice.

This eerily beautiful bar is always open when cruise ships are in port. Otherwise, opening hours are 11am to 11pm between June1st and Augusts 31st and from 6pm to 10pm during the winter season. The entrance fee is NOK 195 (£17.70, $23.00, €20.20).

About 12 miles (20 kms) southwest of Svolvaer is the picturesque fishing village of Henningsvaer, photographs of which feature in countless websites, brochures and blogs.

Sometimes referred to as 'The Venice of Lofoten', the village spans several islets and at the last count had a population of 510 inhabitants. The approach road snakes round the base of the imposing Vågakallen Mountain, arguably one of the most photographed in the world.

The traditional wooden houses are exceptionally well-preserved and the village boasts several quirky shops, cafés and art galleries. It's a good day out. The sea air is clean and bracing, the setting typically mountainous and dramatic.

Buses run approximately every one and a half hours (Line 18-743); the journey takes about 30 minute's and costs approximately £7, $9.10, €8). However, be sure to check the return times of the bus! If the times don't jell, you can take a taxi, which takes about 25 minutes and costs up to £30 ($40, €35) – probably still cheaper than a ship's excursion, if there is one.

Another popular tour is ***Trollfjord***, just 1.25 miles (two kilometres) long; it is in parts only 328 ft (100 metres) wide with steep mountainsides as high as 3,608 ft (1,100 metres).

The fjord is so narrow that most cruise ships simply can't get into the fjord much less turn around at the end of it. Some smaller cruise ships include it in the itinerary, even when it is not formally part of it.

The alternative is to take a tour from Svolvaer. The Trollfjord Cruise company offers trips in both RIB boats and more solid boats. Tours last about three hours and some include fishing and lunch. They all include a search for white tailed eagles (sometimes known as sea eagles).

However, these birds are wild and although you cannot be guaranteed to see them, it is unusual that you don't. Sometimes you can see them really close up. The tours cost NOK 750 (£68, $88, €77), which is not cheap but worth it because it is an experience you are unlikely to forget.

Finally, when you sail out of Svolvaer, don't forget to look back at the statue of the fisherwomen, waving goodbye to those who make their livelihoods from the sea.

***

NARVIK

For anyone who lived through the Second World War, the mere mention of the name Narvik conjures up images of the fjord crammed with warships, running naval battles, amphibious landings and troops hacking out defensive position from the snow.

For those with little or no experience or memory of those days, Narvik is a moderately sized town of some 14,000 people in a municipal area of 781 square miles 2,023 square kilometres) which is home to another 4,000 inhabitants.

It lies at the innermost part of Ofotfjorden, popularly known as Narvik Fjord, a continuation of the great Vestfjord that separates mainland Norway from Lofoten.

So, Narvik enjoys a coastal environment of islands and skerries to the west and is surrounded to the north, east and south by mountains, rising to between 4,900 and 5,600 ft (1,500 and 1,700 metres).

The town's location at the end of the 48-mile (78-kilometre) Ofotfjord, the 18th deepest in Norway with a maximum depth of 1,814 ft (553 meters) ensured that it would become a major port.

During the Second World War, the railway from Narvik to the iron ore mines in Kiruna, Sweden, assumed huge importance for the production of German armaments.

Hitler realised that it was quicker and easier to transport the ore by rail from Sweden to Narvik and thence by sea to Germany, rather than by the more tortuous rail from Sweden through Denmark.

The routing of the iron ore eventually led to bitter winter battles on land and naval battles in the fjord, which was crammed with German warships.

Today, the *Ofot Railway* still transports iron ore from Sweden for shipment abroad.

The most powerful electric locomotives in the world are used to pull 68 wagons, each containing 100 tons of iron ore. There are ten of these trains every day transporting 68,000 tons or ore – enough to make 70,000 cars.

Indeed, at *Riksgränsen,* the border town between Norway and Sweden, car manufacturers test drive new models on the icy roads and frozen lakes.

This practice annually brings industrial photographers to the town, all trying to take shots of the new models, whilst simultaneously causing consternation amongst hotel managers who also cater for disapproving car manufacturing executives.

Although used mainly for transporting ore, passenger trains run several times a day in each direction and from Narvik, tourist trains carry cruise passengers and tourists 27 miles (43 kilometres) to the Swedish border and back.

Riksgränsen

Back in the mid-1700s, when the Sami people discovered iron ore in Swedish Lapland, they used reindeer to carry the ore to the coast. It was not until 1869 that engineers floated the idea of building a railway to do the job. Nearly 30 years later, the Norwegian parliament finally decided the Ofotbanen should be built.

Migrant workers from Norway and Sweden, known as 'navvies', were called in and as construction of the railway progressed, they built small villages alongside it. The atmosphere was not dissimilar from the Klondyke with scores of bars and hundreds or rowdy workers.

The railway was finally opened in 1903.

Today, a tourist train makes a couple of journeys a day at a cost of £5.00 ($6.45, €5.70) each way, passing through impressive and uninhabited mountain scenery, and is often a listed excursion on cruise ships. The journey time is approximately 50 minutes.

For the best viewpoint in Narvik, take the *Cable Car (Fjellheisstasjon)* on Fjellveien, which is open Monday to Friday 12am until 8pm and at weekends from 10 am until 5pm. It costs NOK 295 (£26.75, $34.70, €30.45) for the round trip.

In summer, this is the best place to see the midnight sun. In winter, the views of the fjord surrounded by snow-capped mountains are even more spectacular, especially when the Northern Lights are flaring.

Throughout Norway, there are dozens of war museums documenting the German occupation, but the interactive *Narvik War Museum* has a different concept in that it studies the 'why' and 'how' of warfare.

Indeed, the concept is entitled 'Peacefront'

There are both permanent and temporary exhibitions spread over three floors, so be prepared to spend a couple of hours here – it is a fascinating place.

The exhibitions are based primarily on the German attack on Narvik and Norway in 1940 and the occupation generally, but there is much more than that, including a large section dealing with such issues as conflict, human rights and the futility of war.

The museum at (Kongens gate 39) is open Monday to Sunday between 10am and 4pm. Tickets cost NOK 100 ($9.06, $ 22.75, €10.30) with no concessions for seniors.

Close by is an extraordinary mirrored obelisk that always attracts a lot of attention from visitors and photographers. It is just one of a series of sculptures in the town.

The *Museum Nord, Narvik* focusses on the history of the iron ore harbour, the construction of the Ofoten

railway and the navvies who built it, as well as how Narvik has evolved over the past 100 years.

The museum is located at Administrasjonsveien 3 (Administration Road) in a large brick house built in 1902 and is considerably more interesting than its address, which suggests a paucity of inspiration to say the least.

This dearth of imagination is common in Scandinavia, where many town planners' gift whole sections of towns with names following an uninspiring theme. Thus, Tobaksgatan, Cigaretveien, Pipersgatan etc. (Tobacco Street, Cigarette Road, Pipers Road etc.). How long before we get Cancer Street, one wonders!

Museum Nord is also worth a visit for the view over the town and harbour. It is open between 10am and 4pm on weekdays and 12-3pm at weekends between June 15 and August 16. During the winter months, it is open on Mondays, Wednesdays and Fridays from 10am until 4pm on weekdays and 11am to 4pm at weekends.

The entry fee is NOK 65 (£5.85, $7.60, €6.70) with a NOK 20 discount for seniors.

Travel and tour companies in Narvik also offer RIB Fjord tours in summer and dog sledging, Northern Lights hunting trips and reindeer tours.

For those so inclined, there is a ten-pin bowling centre with 10 bowling alleys, 2 billiard tables, an Air Hockey machine, a children's playground and a fast food outlet serving pizza, burgers, hotdogs, chips, sausages, mineral water and coffee.

The bowling centre is situated at Frydenlundsgata 15 and is open during the winter months from 10am until midnight Monday to Friday and 12 – midnight on Sunday. In summer, the hours are 4pm to midnight every day.

Fiskehallen (The Fish Market) at 42 Kongens gate) is worth a visit and, perhaps, lunch. It is no longer a market, in fact, but a fully licensed restaurant situated in the old market hall building in the centre of the city. The menu includes a variety of fresh fish and seafood dishes, some traditional north Norwegian cuisine, others with a more modern twist.

The restaurant is open for lunch and dinner, and advertises that it is also open 'after hours, Drinks'. Whether that means they have a licence for drinks after hours is open to question.

But, as they say in cruise speak, whatever you do in Narvik – have a great time!

***

HARSTAD AND THE INNER PASSAGE

The Norwegian travel websites like to refer to Harstad as the 'Cultural Capital of the North' and claim it is also 'known' as the 'Gourmet City of the North'. They then advise you to go kayaking, embark on a whale safari or join in on one of the many diving trips in the Norwegian Sea.

Or, they suggest, you might go island hopping with bike and ferry, join a scuba diving trip to the shipwreck Belgica, go swimming in the waterpark Grottebadet, which is buried deep within the 3,593 ft (1,095 metre) high mountain or perhaps speed across the tranquil waters of the fjord in an RIB (for those not in the know, an RIB is one of those fast rubber dinghies that make a lot of noise!)

In other words, these are not necessarily the kind of 'must do' attractions to suit most cruise passengers of a certain age.

Yet, Harstad is a pleasant enough town to wander around and enjoy the surrounding scenic location. If you are fortunate enough to be there on the right day of the year, you might be able to enjoy the annual Festival of Northern Norway, the Arctic Wine Festival or the music festival, or even what is called the Ilios Festival for New Music, which to older ears may sound a little discordant.

Anna Rogde

Within two or three minutes of stepping off the gangway (assuming your ship is not at anchor), you can see a lovely two masted gaff-schooner called the Anna Rogde, moored against the quayside.

Built in 1868, she is 117.6 ft (35.86 metres) long and a so-called 'open ship', which means you can go on board, take photographs and have a paper cup of coffee costing NOK 20 (£2, $2.35, €2.06). It is a very pleasant way to spend half an hour or so.

With a population of about 30,000, Harstad is one of the larger towns in this part of the world. Archaeologists recently discovered a 3,000-year bronze axe and a bronze collar about 2,600 years old, proving that there was a Bronze Age culture on the Trondenes peninsula, just over a mile and a half north of the city centre.

This was followed by a substantial Iron Age settlement and Trondenes was also a Viking centre of power.

According to the Sagas, King Øystein Magnusson built a wooden stave church on the windswept Trondenes peninsula in AD 1114 and it is likely that there was a small farm church 100 years before that.

In the late 12th century, work began on **Trondenes Church**, which this time was built with stone and dedicated to St. Nicholas, patron saint of seafarers.

Surprisingly, because this is not exactly a cathedral, it took several hundred years to complete.

However, by 1440, it was finished and embellished with a rich interior décor, including many beautiful altar cabinets. The remains of the old wall, once 16 feet (4.86 metres) high, can still be seen.

The church was a significant landowner in medieval times and the stock fish trade provided a considerable income that contributed to the abundant artistic ornamentation in the late 15th and 16th centuries.

One reason the church took so long to build may be that the walls are six feet (two metres) thick, a defence not only against the weather but also to give the impression of a fortress.

From the outside, it doesn't look much, but it is well worth the effort of walking there. Apart from anything else, the setting is wild, interesting and very beautiful, and there is a large café and museum close by, too.

Amazingly, the external walls of the church are still pretty much as they were 750 years ago. Inside, the church is renowned for its rich decorations, including three of seven original Gothic triptychs.

Look closely at the baroque pulpit, too, and you will see there is an hourglass, designed to ensure the priest's sermon was not too long.

Centuries ago, the bells hung from a small tower, which was subsequently destroyed. Today, the bells ring out from a squat stone tower in the graveyard.

You can walk to the church, which takes about 40 minutes (if you don't get lost or find yourself having to walk round a long inner channel), or take a taxi which will have you there in five minutes at a cost of about NOK 110 (£10, $13, €11.40). You could also take the Number 12 bus.

Dotted around the church, there are burial mounds and a 2,000-year-old farm mound.

The Second World War and German occupation also left their mark. Although Harstad was one of the few north Norwegian towns not to suffer extensive damage at the hands of retreating Nazi troops, the Trondenes site was once a prisoner-of-war camp for Russian soldiers.

Information markers in Norwegian, German and English guide visitors to the site where the remains of the camp can still be seen. By February, 1942, some two

million of the 3.3 million Soviet soldiers in German custody had died from starvation, exposure, disease or execution.

In July 1945, a burial site was found containing 1,800 bodies. Of these, 609 had been shot and the rest had starved to death.

Approximately 328 ft (100 metres) from the church is the *Trondenes Historical Centre*, where you can gain an insight into the history of the Harstad region from the Stone Age through the Viking and Middle Ages to the present day. Multimedia, lights, sounds and smells enhance the experience and when you have immersed yourself fully in the culture, there is a gift shop to explore.

There is also a large café where you can buy sandwiches at NOK 55 (£5, $6.45, €5.70) or apply for a mortgage and splash out on delicious waffles with sour cream and strawberry jam.

All you need to do then is to sit on the terrace, enjoy the wonderful views of the fjord and islands, and try to figure out how many months it will take to pay off the cost of the waffles.

Heading back to your ship, the likelihood is that you will sail north to Tromsø. Some ships sail out to sea and take the outer seaward route, which is faster and does not require a pilot (which in Norway costs several thousand pounds/dollars).

Others take what is known as the Inside Passage, a winding, twisting channel which in places is so narrow that you can see into the rooms of the houses on the shore.

Here, too, you may well see the white-tailed sea eagles swooping down to snatch the odd trout or salmon – a wonderful sight to behold!

***

TROMSØ
GATEWAY TO THE ARCTIC

Many years ago, a friend who lived in Tromsø told me that when the 'midnight sun' is shining in summer, people only sleep for 20 minutes or so, three or four times a day. "In winter", he said, "we have a real problem getting people in to work because they will sleep for as long as 18 hours a day if you let them".

The other side of that coin is that tourists who sail to northern Norway often find that it is two or three o'clock in the morning before they feel tired and, horrified, eventually go to bed.

The tourist authorities and local tour companies, of course, cater for both winter and summer occupations so, whatever the season, Tromsø is a busy, thriving city that likes to call itself 'The Gateway to the Arctic'.

In summer, you can go whale watching, kayaking and hiking or on fjord tours, fishing and birdwatching trips.

In winter, Tromsø is one of the best

places in Europe to see the Northern Lights *(Aurora Borealis)* and you can go reindeer and dog sledding, skiing, snowmobiling, ice fishing, snowshoeing or join mountain and fjord scenery tours, photographic tours and culture tours, and see any one or more of a dozen different attractions.

Straddling the island of Tromsø, there is a variety of museums to see, a planetarium, an Arctic Botanical Garden, a Polar Museum, an Arctic Cathedral, a polar aquarium and a cable car to the summit of a mountain offering spectacular views of the city, its mountains and fjords.

This is a city that buzzes. It hosts the Tromsø International Film Festival and the Northern Lights Festival and it has a vibrant nightlife, too, should you be overnighting there.

It is the largest town in northern Norway with a

population of nearly 76,000 and is also larger than any other town or settlement closer to the North Pole. except Murmansk and Norisk in Russia.

Yet, thanks to the warming effect of the Gulf Stream, the climate is milder than many places further south and decidedly warmer than such places as northern Canada and Siberia on the same latitude.

People have lived here for as long as 10,000 years. The Sami people have been here for at least 1,000 years.

The town began life as a fishing village in the Middle Ages, but for centuries the monopoly on the cod trade belonged to Bergen in the south.

In 1794, however, King Christian VII issued Tromsø with a city charter, even though fewer than 100 people lived there at the time. This opened the flood gates and Tromsø soon grew in importance:

It soon became a centre not only for cod fishing but also for Arctic hunting, trading furs and other arctic products as far afield as Archangel and southern Europe.

The city also became a starting point for late 19th century expeditions to the Arctic. Fritjof Nansen, Roald Amundsen and Umberto Nobile all trained in the area and Nansen and Amundsen recruited crews for their expedition ships here.

Research into the Arctic regions also began here. The Aurora Borealis observatory was established in 1927. Today, the University of Tromsø specialises in Arctic and Marine Biology and the Norwegian Polar Institute is a major centre for scientific research, mapping and environmental monitoring in the Arctic and Antarctic. The city is also a major centre for data downloading (from satellites).

Fortunately, Tromsø was relatively unscathed during the Second World War. The German battleship, *Tirpitz* was finally sunk at Kvaløysletta across the fjord due west of Tromsø airport.

The city also received thousands of refugees from other parts of northern Norway where the retreating German forces employed a scorched earth policy, burning everything in their path in order to make life as difficult as possible for advancing Russian troops and to prevent them gaining any advantage.

Later, following a merger with other outlying districts, the population of Tromsø tripled, yet the city has retained its 'old worldly' look and, according to Wikipedia, has the largest number of historic wooden houses north of Trondheim, the oldest of them dating to 1789.

The hub of the city is its main square which looks out to the 3,399 ft (1036 metre) ***Tromsøbrua (Tromsø Bridge*** that links the port and the old town to the mainland. The bridge has 58 spans, of which the longest is 262 ft (80 metres) with a maximum clearance of 125ft (38 metres).

Should you decide to walk across the bridge, be aware that it can be slippery and very windy – and for some, quite vertiginous.

At the far end, is the so-called *Arctic Cathedral,* which is a misnomer because it is actually just a parish church known as *Tromsdalen Church*, the real Cathedral being in the centre of the city.

Built with concrete and aluminium panels, the 'cathedral' was completed in 1965 but seven years later, a glass mosaic was added to the eastern end.

Often likened to the Sydney Opera House, the church is also said to have been built in the shape of a polar bear, although that demands a certain amount of imagination. Others say it resembles an iceberg, which is more realistic but probably not the intention of the architect, Jan Inge Hovig.

What is so appealing about the church is its simplicity and wonderful light. There is very little in the way of ornamentation and this gives the interior a greater sense of spirituality and tranquillity.

The real *Tromsø (Lutheran) Cathedral,* built in 1861 is Norway's only wooden cathedral. Located at 70° North, it is probably the northernmost Protestant cathedral in the world. It has seating for more than 600 worshippers, although these days no doubt the clergy have a job finding them as most Norwegians go to church only for the occasional midnight service at

Christmas or to be christened, married or bid farewell to this mortal coil.

The distinctive church, built in the Gothic revival style, lies just off *Sjøgata (Sea Street)*, the main shopping street.

An earlier church on the site, built in 1711, was replaced in 1803 by a new church, which in turn was moved to make room for the present church.

The cathedral was consecrated in December 1861 and a year later the bell tower was completed. It was another 20 years, however, before the interior decorations and art were completed.

Not far from the Arctic 'Cathedral', The *Fjellheisen (Cable Car),* runs from Solliveien at sea level to the top of Storsteinen mountain 1,381 ft (421 metres) above the fjord. Arguably, the most popular attraction in Tromsø, the viewing platform at the upper station affords spectacular views of Tromsø and the surrounding mountains, islands and fjords.

There are two gondolas, each carrying 28 passengers, and there is a fully licensed restaurant. At the summit. It makes a great place to have dinner when the cloud base is high, especially in winter when there is a high chance of seeing the Northern Lights.

The cable car operates between 10 am and 11pm in winter (1st August to 31st May) and between 10am and 01.00 am during the summer season.

Return tickets cost NOK 210 (£18.80, $24.40, €21.50). There are no concessions for seniors.

Back on Tromsø Island, cruise ships berth in one of two places. Smaller ships, including the Hurtigruten, dock within 100 yards of the city centre. Larger ships are further north on the eastern side of Tromsø Island.

Close to the latter berth, is the ***Arctic Alpine Botanical Garden***, which is a great venue because there are no fees, no fences and no gates, and the garden is open year-round.

This is home to thousands of plant species from all

over the world. There are separate sections showcasing plants from the Himalayas, South America and South Africa, but the emphasis is on Arctic and Antarctic plants, including the famous – and quite stunning, blue poppy (*Meconopsis grandis*).

Further up the hill, at Hansine Hansens veg 17, is the ***Northern Lights Planetarium.*** Here you can sit in the 95-seat full dome theatre and watch superb displays of the Northern Lights (Aurora Borealis) even in summer!

As part of the Science Centre of Northern Norway and Tromsø University, the Planetarium also stages a series of shows transporting visitors to the moon, constellations and journeys through the solar system and distant galaxies.

T

Lego boxes at The Science Centre

The Science Centre comprises nearly 100 interactive exhibits for the curious-minded of all ages. To get there you can either walk up the hill from the botanical garden, or take the No. 20, 21, 32 or 33/34 bus from the city centre.

Admission, which includes the Science Centre, is NOK 120 (£10.75, $13.95, €12.30) with a NOK 30 discount for seniors. The venue is open Monday to Sunday from 11am until 4pm year round.

Returning to the city centre, the ***Tromsdalen Library (Bibliotek)*** on Anton Jakobsensvei 1, just off the main square, is a useful place to visit as it offers free wi-fi. Indeed, every library in Norway has free wi-fi.

The main square is an attraction in itself, with views of the harbour, the bridge and the Arctic Cathedral. On most days there are marketstalls, some displaying Sami hats, boots, sweaters and utensils made from reindeer horns, others selling fresh fish and shellfish caught that morning by the crews of fishing boats moored down on the waterfront.

Statue of fisherman in Tromsø main square

If you walk down to the waterfront and turn left, past the old wooden houses, you will find in a red wharf house from 1837, the ***Polar Museum.***

It is not large but it is endlessly fascinating, focussing on Tromsø as the jumping off point for Arctic explorers and a centre for Arctic seal hunting. Covering a diverse selection of subjects, the museum is a mine of information about Nansen and Amundsen, William Barentz, whaling in the 17th and 18th centuries, trappers in Svalbard and much more.

Although the museum boasts many original artefacts and model dioramas, most of the text is in Norwegian. Also, if you are tall, do look out for the overhead beams. They have been padded but can still give you a nasty surprise.

Certain aspects covered by the museum, such as seal hunting in the Arctic ocean and whale hunting, may upset some visitors today, but perhaps they should focus more on the fact that the museum is representing the activities of yesteryear and that history cannot be deleted just because attitudes and morals have changed.

Trappers cabin in Svalbard – diorama at the Polar Museum

This is an absorbing museum, beautifully presented and one of the top ten attractions in Tromsø. It is absolutely worth the entrance fee of NOK 70 (£6.25, $8.15, €7.20) with a half-price concession for seniors.

The museum is open from 11am–7 pm in the winter months (1st August–14th June) and from 9am-6pm during the rest of the year, except for 1st of May and Norway's National day on 17th May.

Another small but equally fascinating museum is the **Tromsø Museum** at Lars Thoringsvei 10, which conveys a surprising amount of information, not least by focussing on Norway's history of mistreating its Sami minority. It does this with considerably more honesty than many other establishments, which prefer to sweep this aspect of Norwegian history under the carpet.

The museum offers exhibitions and events covering Sami culture and the northern lights to dinosaurs and church art. The entrance fee is just NOK

60 (£5.40, $6.95, €6.15 and seniors half price) with opening hours much the same as other museums, according to the season.

Meanwhile, **The Northern Norway Art Museum's** permanent collection comprises paintings, drawings, sculptures, videos, textiles and handicrafts. It was voted Museum of the Year in 2017 and encourages 'reflection, play and exploration and, in so doing, enhances our perspectives of the North'.

Constantly evolving, the permanent collection displays artworks by Munch, Hockney and other leading Swedish and Norwegian artists, including Sami artists.

Open daily from 10am until 5pm year-round, the admission fee is NOK 80 (£7.20, $ 9.30, €8.20).

One museum that is often overlooked is the **Perspective Museum (Perspektivet Museet)** housed in a magnificent neoclassical building from 1838. It is located on the main shopping street, Storgata (No. 95) and is a real gem, exhibiting photographs of the city's past and present from an archive of approximately half a million images.

To begin with, it is tempting merely to scan the photographs, but gradually they become compelling and often thought provoking as the lives of townspeople, fisherfolk and Sami reindeer herders, for example, are gradually revealed.

It is a riveting and relaxing way to spend an hour or so. There is a small library, and a 'mini' café selling small snacks and coffee. Admission is free but donations are received gratefully. The museum is open daily except for the Christmas and New Year holidays, 1st may, 17th may, Good Friday and Easter Sunday.

Polaria is an Arctic themed 'experience centre' with several films depicting the Northern Lights, the island of Spitzbergen in the Svalbard archipelago and the Arctic wilderness in a five-screen multi-media cinema.

An 'Arctic' walkway leads you past displays of stuffed animals, equipment from polar expeditions and numerous small tanks containing fish, crabs and other crawling things from rock pools, and then on to an open pool that is home to bearded seals from Spitzbergen.

There are some 'shows' but these are not primarily intended to be for the public's entertainment, rather than a means of keeping the seals fit and healthy. The public, nonetheless are always entertained.

Billed as the 'world's most northerly aquarium' (everything in this part of the world is the 'most northerly'), Polaria opened in May 1998 and is designed as an educational experience, especially for children.

A seal hunting ship, the *Polstjerna (meaning the 'Pole Star)* is housed approximately 75-100 yards away in a separate building, although on every single visit I have made to Tromsø, it has always been closed.

Bearded seal

Perhaps, that is not so important given that there are so many other places to see and experience in a wonderfully vibrant city.

***

ALTA, MASI AND ALTAFJORD

Alta is a winter port. Ships go there because the surrounding countryside is arguably the best place in Europe to view the Northern Lights and you are unlikely to find anywhere else along the coast that is as close to the heart of the Sami culture.

Like Tromsø, there are companies that specialise in tracking the phase of the lights and their intensity, and the most likely places to see them on any given night, whether on the coast, in Alta itself or in one of several venues.

If the cloud base is low in the Alta region, coaches will take you to venues close to the coast or even the Finnish border where the skies maybe clearer.

The guides will always give you options, a realistic assessment of the chances of seeing the lights and the opportunity to opt out of excursions if need be.

Naturally, even with this kind of expertise, the lights are not always visible and sometimes appear a light grey colour as opposed to the intense greens, yellows and reds in professional photographs. That's because the camera can see colours that are not visible to the human eye.

So, it is always a matter of luck and when you *are* lucky, you will remember the lights of that night for the rest of your life.

Alta is also a winter port of call because of the staggering beauty of the Altafjord and the excursions available in the region.

The first impressions of many cruise ship passengers are that Alta has nothing much to offer. It may look deserted when your shuttle bus arrives there. That's because the temperature may be as low as minus 15°-20° and the residents are either in their homes, out skiing or in one of the many indoor shopping and restaurant malls.

First impressions, of course, are all too often misleading. Alta, in fact, is a fascinating town. In terms of area, it is the seventh largest municipality in Norway with a population of nearly 21,000.

Rock carvings date back to between 4,200BC to 500BC and prove that Sami people were hunting, herding reindeer and skiing here way back in history. There has been a *Sami Market* in the centre of Alta since the late 1400s. It became an 'official' market in 1836 and lasts for three days every December and March.

Here, Sami people sell everything from cooked reindeer meat, knives with bone handles made from reindeer horns and reindeer fur hats to colourful woolly slippers, sweaters, antlers, pelts and all things Sami.

Known as the *Bossekop market*, it was the main place for the mountain Sami to trade mountain goods for

coastal products, for instance, reindeer pelts, meal, grouse, ptarmigan and fish etc., for flour, butter, salt, wool and other textiles, not to mention coffee and tobacco.

The market was itinerant like the semi-nomadic Sami themselves, so Alta was just one of the locations in which it was set up – Tromsø, Hammerfest and Honningsvåg and Kautokeino to name but a few.

Moreover, the market was always financially successful. Back in the late 1800s, it was turning over the equivalent of more than six million Norwegian crowns, which in today's money would be about £540,000 ($700,000, €620,000). How much it turns over today is not recorded.

In March each year, the town hosts an *International Ice Carving Festival* in the main square, which for several days resounds with the buzz of chain saws. Here, you can wander amongst dragons, monsters, children's play houses made of ice and an open-air ice theatre. If you are lucky, you may also be treated to free waffles at one of the stalls.

One of the unmissable, not to say unforgettable 'bucket list' excursions from Alta is to the Sorrisniva Igloo Hotel.

Welcome bar at the Sorrisniva Igloo Hotel – Blue curacao and vodka? Served in ice glasses, of course.

Needless to say, it claims to be the world's northernmost ice hotel, built from scratch each year and always with a different theme. This is necessary because, come Spring, the hotel simply melts away...

The hotel consists of two buildings – one built with snow and ice containing superb ice sculptures and an ice bar; the other a warm, wooden building with a living room and traditional, licensed Norwegian restaurant serving an á la carte menu. (don't forget to bring gold bars with you!)

The owners first built the hotel in 1999 and were the first in Norway to build a structure entirely of ice and snow. Indeed, there was only one other in the world.

Today, local workers and artists use 250 tons of ice and 7,000 cubic metres of snow, all taken from the valley and its river.

With 26 bedrooms, four 'decorated suites', an ice bar, lots of ice carvings and sculptures, the hotel even boasts its own chapel and, remarkably, takes only four to five weeks to build.

Just in case you are wondering – the fire is fake!

No matter how snug and warm the hotel may be with double reindeer skins as a mattress and heavy-duty sleeping bags on offer, most cruise passengers will prefer to return to the ship for their night's sleep and, in the view of the author, that is a good decision.

That's because there is no toilet in the igloo hotel, so if you are of a certain age when such visits are required at night, you would have to walk across the frozen ground to the wooden building some yards away.

This does not seem a particularly attractive proposition, when temperatures outside could be as low as minus 10-15°C (14-5°F) or more!

No, a day trip is the ideal alternative and an absolutely fascinating excursion on which to partake.

The other 'bucket list' attraction is a coach trip to the *Village of Masi*. The threat to flood the village and effectively destroy the Sami culture is discussed in detail in *The Sami of Lapland* chapter on page 27 of this book.

Suffice to say here that this is a fascinating and stunningly beautiful two-hour journey through the interior of Lapland, past ice waterfalls, frozen lakes and snowy mountains.

At Masi, visitors can meet genuine Sami (as opposed to 'tourist' Sami), who will take you reindeer sledding, a truly wonderful experience in the wild.

Dog sledding, too, is increasingly popular in the Alta region and the *Finnmarksløpet – Europe's longest sled dog race* starts from the main square in Alta on the Saturday of the 10th week of the year.

This 745-mile (1,200-km) long race attracts mushers from all over Europe and more than 1,500 dogs each year and the gruelling course takes five to six days to complete. That is in good weather!

As temperatures usually fall in good weather, this can create problems; the record low temperature during the race being minus 44°.

The mushers stop only at designated checkpoints and for obligatory rest breaks, so some teams are driving at all times.

It is a phenomenal test of strength and mental character, and even when the mushers and their teams of 14 dogs reach the end of each stage, they must tend to the dogs first before resting themselves.

So taxing is the race that only about half the teams complete the full distance from Alta to Kirkenes near the Russian border and back. Consequently, there is now a 310-mile (500-km) race run with teams of eight dogs, as well.

Teams of veterinarians carry out health checks at the checkpoints and if any dogs are showing signs of exhaustion or stress, they must be retired. If too many dogs in a team show these signs, the musher must retire the entire team. Conditions being what they often are, there are very seldom any arguments about the decision.

The town of Alta comprises three villages – Bossekop, Elvebakken and Bukta, the main part of Alta being in Bossekop.

From your ship's berth, a shuttle bus will normally take you through all three villages with the first stopping point at the *World Heritage Rock Art Museum*, otherwise known as the *Alta Museum*. This is just over three miles (five kilometres) west of 'downtown' Alta. The shuttle bus then continues directly to the centre of town.

Stopping off at the museum is a good idea, firstly because there is an excellent café with stunning views of the fjord, secondly because the museum stages various fascinating exhibitions about the history and culture of the region and thirdly because it also houses some of the rock carvings found at five locations close to the museum.

The Museum café and, below, the view from it.

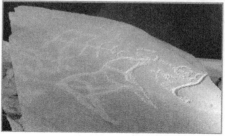

The main rock carvings, dating 2,000 to 6,200 years old, can only be seen in the summer months, when there is no snow but, as mentioned previously, there are examples of them in the museum itself. There is also a museum shop selling high quality souvenirs, books, cards and Sami products.

The museum opens at different times depending on the season but is always open when a cruise ship is in port – except during the Christmas period and on New Year's Eve and New Year's Day.

The entrance fee in summer (May 1st to September 30th) is NOK 120 (£10.75, $13.90, €12.30) and during the rest of the year NOK 80 (£7.20, $9.25, €8.20). There is a marginal discount for seniors of NOK 10 in summer and NOK 5 at other times.

Approximately 12.5 miles (20 kms) from Alta, at Kåfjord, a little further on from the Alta Museum, is the small and privately-owned *Tirpitz Museum.* Evan, the owner, lives in Oslo but opens the museum from mid-May to mid-August.

He is a fund of knowledge about the German battleship and the museum is crammed with authentic artefacts, personal items from the crew and memorabilia from it, including uniforms, models, radio equipment, sections of anchor chain, photographs and so on.

Some 20,000 German troops were stationed at Alta during the Second World War and the port was the largest German naval base outside Germany at that time. *Tirpitz* alone had a crew of nearly 2,000 men.

Churchill, recognising that the battleship, which he called 'The Beast', posed a huge threat to the British-American Arctic convoys transporting food, arms and ammunition to the Russians in Murmansk.

He ordered countless bombing raids to be flown with the objective of sinking her, all to no avail.

Having been attacked in Trondheim fjord, Hitler ordered *Tirpitz* to Kåfjord, where she was protected by anti-submarine nets and smoke generators in the mountains. Despite these, three British X-craft mini-submarines managed to penetrate the nets in September, 1943.

By attaching high explosives to her hull, the British circumvented the upper armour-plated parts of the hull and put her out of action for six months.

After that, the ship was ordered to Tromsø fjord, where she was ultimately sunk by British bombers, one of which scored a direct hit with the massive Tallboy bomb travelling at the speed of sound from 10,000 feet.

Tirpitz has since been dismantled and is no longer at the site of the sinking.

Finally, back in Alta, the **Northern Lights Cathedral**, an elegant architectural triumph, is a delight to see.

Clad in shimmering titanium, the exterior – built in the shape of a spiral leading up to a belfry, reflects the sunlight – and also the green colouring of the Aurora as the lights flicker across the sky.

At the entrance, Jacob's ladder reaches towards the belfry and the eye is drawn to a bronze figure of Christ at the altar.

Thanks to its simplicity and stunning design, the interior is simple, beautiful and very moving.

The cathedral seats approximately 350 people. There was some contention as to whether it was a cathedral at all rather than just a parish church, but the bishop who consecrated it in 2013 observed that there were precedents, notably the Arctic Cathedral in Tromsø and Lofoten Cathedral. "A Bishop," he remarked, "is at home in all churches".

It's not a bad way to end the day, with perhaps a silent prayer for a really vibrant display of the Aurora in the evening.

**

HAMMERFEST

The contest for being the 'world's most northerly town begins to hot up in Hammerfest, which lies a little south of Honningsvåg, which also claims the title.

Unfortunately for Honningsvåg, it has a population of only 2,484 and Norwegian law dictates that a 'town' must have at least 5,000 residents. Hammerfest, on the other hand, has a population of 8,052 and received town status in 1789.

The discussion does not end there, though, because Honningsvåg was actually officially declared a city (despite its minute population) in 1996 and the law stating that a town or city must have more than 5,000 residents was not passed until 1997.

So, the 'northernmost' title is clearly still up for grabs.

Looking at a globe, it may be that neither Hammerfest nor Honningsvåg are the northmost towns. That honour probably goes to Longyearbyen on the island of Spitzbergen in the Svalbard archipelago.

Except that Longyearbyen is described as a town, whereas in 1996, Honningsvåg was declared a 'city'.

In any event, it is certainly further north than Hammerfest. The question is; does it really matter?

Greater Hammerfest is a municipality spanning three large islands, only one of which is connected to the rest of Norway by a bridge.

Hammerfest town is a major northern port with an ice-free harbour, which back in the Stone Age made it an important fishing and Arctic hunting settlement.

The people of Hammerfest traded with Russia from as far back as the Viking age, and by the 1760s, Russia was shipping grain to the town in return for fish.

Later, the Russians paid for fish with roubles, which at that time were used quite widely as currency throughout northern Norway and as far south as Bodø.

Today, Hammerfest is still an important fishing port and a centre for processing natural gas from a gas field in the Barents Sea. In summer, cruise ships bring some 20,000 tourists to the town.

In 1856, a hurricane blew most of the buildings down, then in 1890, fire raced through the town, destroying 65% of its buildings. But like a phoenix, the city rose again and during its reconstruction Hammerfest became the first town in northern Europe to have electric street lighting.

The town was ravaged once more during the embers of the Second World War. German warships were based in the harbour from 1940, but subsequently either left or were sunk.

In 1944, German bombers destroyed several streets in the town and ships in the harbour, an act that marked the beginning of the German scorched earth policy of retreat, systematically razing to the ground every building, every installation, every house from Kirkenes close to the Soviet border and throughout northern Norway.

With only one building left standing in Hammerfest, the population was evacuated forcibly. Today, that building is the oldest building in the town. It is the funeral chapel.

Those bleak days are commemorated in the **Museum of Reconstruction (Gjenreisningsmuseet),** at Kirkegata 19, with many photographs and authentic artefacts depicting just how desperate the returning residents were, trying to rebuild their houses and shops with only the most basic means.

Aware that the German troops were approaching, many residents buried treasured items in their gardens. One of the most poignant exhibits is an authentic American barbershop chair.

The local barber, who had acquired this from Chicago prior to the war, wrapped it in tarpaulin and buried it, then dug it up after the war. He later donated it to the museum.

The museum shows how slowly the town developed. First people built one room houses and only gradually added more rooms. Furnishings were extremely basic and it was not until the 1950s that there was any kind of choice, not just of furniture and furnishings, but also clothing.

The museum is open Monday-Friday from 10am – 3pm and at weekends from 11am 0 2pm. The entrance fee is NOK 80 (£7.15, $9.20, €8.15) with a NOK 30 discount for seniors.

The museum lies in the upper reaches of the town and its tower is one of the taller and more distinctive structures in Hammerfest, with a special photographic gallery affording panoramic views of the town.

The best views, however, are to be seen from the summit of **Mount Tyven,** at 1,371 ft (418-metres). An eight-kilometre (five-mile) dirt road winds along the ridge of the mountain through some spectacular mountain scenery and up to the tundra *(Vidda)* that stretches all the sway to Siberia.

If that is too strenuous, the **Salen Hill Lookout Point** offers pretty much the same views but from a lower height of 282 feet (86 metres).

There are two ways to reach the viewpoint. The first is along a zigzag path *(Sikksakksveien)* which is steep but short and takes about 20 minutes if you are reasonably fit and mobile. The path begins at the blue pavilion in the town centre.

The other way is to skirt round the mountain, walking from the port up Nybakken and then turning right onto Idrettsveien.

This is by far the more interesting route and gives you a better insight into life in Hammerfest during the winter months, with avalanche breaks immediately above many of the houses.

After walking along Idrettsveien for a while, you

will come to a yellow wooden house with a gravel path passing uphill to the right of it. This takes you to the top of the

Salen hill.

As you wend your way along the track, up between the houses, you may well see wild reindeer grazing on the nutrient rich grasses, as well as excellent views across the lake.

Once you climb above the houses, you find yourself up on the tundra, carpeted with tiny alpine flowers and in some of the marshy areas cotton grass.

At the top of the Salen hill, with the centre of Hammerfest spread below you, is **Mikkelgammen,** a Sami hut built of peat.

Sami reindeer herders traditionally live in tents of skin (*lavoo* in Norwegian, *kåta* in Swedish Samiland) when following the migrating herds.

The peat huts are more permanent dwellings used for centuries.

Although Mikkelgammen is obviously a tourist attraction, it is nonetheless the closest you can get to the real Sami experience other than travelling with the reindeer herders during the migration.

That is partly due to the location, right on the edge of the tundra, which lends the huts a feeling of being miles away from anywhere in uninhabited territory. It is also due to the hosts actually living here.

Many cruise ships include Mikkelgammen as a ship's excursion and that is certainly the easiest and perhaps the only way to get there for passengers who have mobility difficulties.

On arrival, you will be welcomed either in one of the smaller peat huts, where you will sit on reindeer pelts around a roaring fire, or in the larger communal hut where you will be served coffee, reindeer meat and other delicacies, also round a roaring fire.

Back in the town, it is worth stopping off at the **Protestant Church of Hammerfest,** which replaced the previous church burned down during the German retreat.

The church was consecrated in 1961 and designed by Hans Magnus, who also designed – you've guessed it – the northernmost church in the world on Spitzbergen in the Svalbard archipelago.

The elongated triangular design represents both the Holy Trinity and the racks used for drying stock fish. The interior wooden ceiling is redolent of an upturned boat.

Immediately outside the cruise terminal is the **Polar Bear Museum,** run by **Royal and Ancient Polar Bear Society (Isbjørnsklubben).**

While some people may find stuffed animals unappealing, the museum is nonetheless worth a visit because it displays a rich history of the polar regions, arctic fishing, hunting and exploration.

Here, you can become a member in the Royal and Ancient Polar Bear Society. It used to be that membership was restricted to those who had led or been a part of an arctic expedition, but the Museum clearly ran out of money, so now you can buy membership for NOK 220 (£19.70, $25.30, €22.40).

(I am happy to assert that I travelled by snowmobile and dog team from Resolute Bay up the Wellington Channel, crossing the neck of Devon Island and along the Jones Sound to Grisefjord in Ellesmere Island So although I did buy my membership (for £10), I feel I would almost certainly have been accepted as a member under the original terms).

The one-off fee helps to support the exhibitions and pay for the elements of membership, which gives you a small polar bear enamel pin in silver casing, a sticker with the club's logo, a brochure and a diploma signed by the Mayor of Hammerfest. You also receive a membership card, guaranteed access to the AGM and a 10 per cent discount in the souvenir shop for all goods except postcards and stamps.

Hammerfest is a fun town. In winter, you can go ice fishing, snowmobiling, and chase the Aurora. In summer, there are any number of outdoor activities.

That said, the weather is not always sunny. Just outside the harbour, the Norwegian Sea begins to merge into the Barents Sea and, as anybody who knows about the wartime Arctic convoys will tell you, it can be freezing cold out there and more than a little choppy.

This was never better illustrated than one summer in the mid-1990s, when SilverSea Cruises offered a 'Silversea Experience' in Hammerfest; to join a local fishing boat and sail out to a sea brimming with record-sized cod, salmon and halibut.

The 'visitnorway.com' website describes the experience thus: 'The summer months are the prime season, when both locals and visitors make the most of the warm temperatures and light evenings. Go above the Arctic Circle to get the ultimate outdoors adventure under the midnight sun.'

This was like a magnet for the 'tough guys' on the cruise, but although the SilverSea experience took place at height of summer, the weather changed suddenly and those who had signed up for the experience got more than they had bargained for; they were out there for several hours in sleet and snow, freezing their nuts off.

When they arrived back on the ship, they looked like little boys who had been forced to stay out in the snow in minus temperatures during school playtime.

They were shivering and blue with cold, and they only caught two medium sized fish between them, which just goes to show that even fish feel the cold.

***

HONNINGSVÅG AND THE NORTH CAPE.

Honningsvåg is one of the smallest cities in Norway, but with the largest port in northern Norway. Only 2,484 people live there year-round and apart from fishing, walking, hiking, kayaking, bird watching and breathing the pure, sweet sea air, there is not a great deal to do or see there.

Between 80 and 100 cruise ships visit Honningsvåg each year with the average cruise ship having a larger passenger population than the city itself.

The astute reader will notice that I refer to Honningsvåg as a 'city' despite its small population and the fact that Norwegian law states that there must be at least 5,000 inhabitants to become a town or city.

As explained in the previous chapter, that law was passed in 1997 and because of its Hammerfest claimed the title of 'northernmost city/town in Europe'. However, in 1996, the authorities declared Honningsvåg a city – and therefore (a) is not affected by the law and (b) also claims the 'northernmost' title.

Honningsvåg is an important port not only because it has a deep-water harbour and five piers within five minutes of the city centre and can handle four large cruise ships simultaneously, but because it is also the jumping off port for the *North Cape (Nordkapp)*.

Contrary to popular opinion, the *North Cape (Nordkapp)* is *not* the northernmost part of Europe, rather than the northernmost point to which one can *drive* in Europe, being the terminus for

European highway, E69.

The furthest north title for Europe is a headland called *Kinnarrodden* otherwise known as *Cape NordKinn* a little less than a mile (1,500 metres) further west along the coast at 71° 08'02" N by 27°39'00" E.

Some ships merely sail round the North Cape, with passengers gazing up at the 1,007 ft (307-metre) clifftop whilst others run coach excursions there. Both are interesting, the former because of the plethora of puffins skimming at speed across the surface of the water where the Atlantic Ocean meets the Barents Sea, the latter because the North Cape complex is a highly developed tourist attraction.

Years ago, when I expressed a desire to go there, somebody said: "Oh, you don't want to do that. The North Cape is just one big shop". I replied: "I do want to go there, actually, because I want to be the one who says it is just one big shop!"

So, what does a coach trip to the North Cape entail and what can you expect to see when you get there?

Firstly the 22.4-mile (36-kilometre) journey takes you across the tundra or *vidda* which stretches all the way east to Siberia and on the way you have a fair chance of seeing wild reindeer and the odd, token Sami with a couple of reindeer at the side of the road hoping for a passing car to stop and take photographs for a small donation. Or a big one, for that matter.

On arrival, visitors will see a huge car park crammed with campervans, cars and coaches, so the walk to the Visitor's Centre and North Cape marker may be a longish one and very possibly a cold and windy one.

Even at the height of summer, the weather can be harsh. Passengers on the SilverSea cruise mentioned in the previous chapter on Hammerfest, arrived at the North Cape in mid-June in a blizzard, with snow being blown horizontally across the plateau and visibility down to about 25 metres. There is also a fair chance of being engulfed in fog with no views on offer at all.

In good weather, however, visitors will be able to stare across the empty ocean and ruminate on the fact that only the Svalbard archipelago stands in the way of a clear view to the North Pole 1,306-miles (2,101-kms) to the north.

They will also be able to see the midnight sun skimming the horizon (at midnight!) between mid-May and the end of July, and the Northern Lights in winter if the sky is clear and they are in evidence.

The Visitor Centre is a hive of activity; some 200,000 tourists arrive there each year, most of them having come through Honningsvåg.

There is an observation room, a cinema showing multi-media films of the midnight sun, the aurora and a look at life in the region throughout the year.

There is also a 'Cave of Lights', a large restaurant and a café, a chapel and, believe it or not, a small Thai museum.

This commemorates the visit by King Chulalongkom (Rama V) in July 1907. Several kings, presidents and other worthy people from Britain, Germany and France have been to the North Cape, including King Oscar II of Norway and Sweden who arrived there in July 1873 and declared 'So, the Kingdom of Norway reaches to here'.

A small obelisk marks the occasion and the King's comment that it was intended "not as a transitory adornment, but as a solemn sign that the Kingdom of Norway reaches hither…"

What else is there to see at the North Cape? Oh yes – a huge shop!

Visitors to the North Cape arriving under their own steam should be aware that the entrance fee is a whopping NOK 285 (£25.60, $32.92, €29.20). This includes parking, the panorama film, historical exhibitions and the Cave of Lights, souvenir shops, restaurants and cafés for 24 hours.

The high fees have been a matter of some discussion for the best part of a decade, but the company that runs the attraction point out that the operation, maintenance and security do not come cheaply.

Whether the fee is worth what is on offer is open to question and one has only to visit Tripadvisor to see the various comments.

At the end of the day, though, the North Cape is a 'bucket list' attraction that you are only likely to visit once.

Honningsvåg, however, is a delightful city in which to spend a few hours walking, shopping, taking photographs and enjoying the harbour, the few attractions and the surrounding countryside.

Here, colourful houses huddle together as if trying to shelter from the weather as they climb higher up the mountain, shielded by metal barriers to protect them against rock falls and, worse, avalanches in winter.

Most of the attractions in the town are within a few minutes walk from the ship's berth. Immediately outside the fenced off cruise quays, there is a large, state-run tourist shop fronted by a suitably ugly troll, which is the subject of more photographers and selfie-seekers than the North Cape!

The shop is as well stocked as in any other port and there are some good buys if you are interested in wild weather clothing.

For souvenirs, I always recommend a small wooden Sami shop just around the corner (just turn right and right again and it is the last building in the row). You can see it easily by the reindeer antlers outside.

The shop is run by two delightful Sami who may well ask to borrow your binoculars to see if they can spot their husbands and the family reindeer on the *vidda* high above the town.

Sami people tend to be quite small.
Edward, however, is 6ft 7ins tall!

Any profits from your purchases here go directly into the Sami economy rather than into the state coffers at the main tourist store. Incidentally, never ask Sami people how many reindeer they own. It is equivalent to asking how much somebody earns and is deeply hurtful to them.

In the small square (***Holmen),*** there is a statue of a St. Bernard's dog called ***Bamse***, which means 'Teddy Bear 'in Norwegian.

Bamse is a very special dog. His story begins in Oslo, where a visiting whaling captain, Erling Hafto, bought him in 1937. From then on, Bamse lived on board except when Hafto's ship was moored in Honningsvåg, where the dog was remembered as standing guard when the local children played.

When war broke out, The Royal Norwegian Navy commissioned Captain Harfto's boat, *Thorodd,* as a costal patrol ship and thus, Bamse officially became a member of the crew.

His story evolved in a similar way to that of Just Nuisance, a Great Dane who became the only dog ever to be officially enlisted into the British Royal Navy and was so named because he liked to lie and sun himself at the top of the gangway, where he was, indeed, a nuisance because of his size.

After the German invasion and occupation of

Norway in April 1940, Captain Hafto managed to escape with his ship to Britain. Based in Rosyth and stationed in Montrose, she was eventually converted to a minesweeper.

Bamse, now a seasoned sailor, was a great favourite with the crew who said he cheered them up when they were low, not least when he would stand in the bow next to the gun position wearing a metal helmet that the crew had made for him during sea battles.

When the ship was berthed in Montrose, Bamse became renowned for saving the commanding officer of another ship from a man attacking him with a knife. Bamse intervened and pushed the assailant into the harbour.

On another occasion, he saved a sailor who had fallen overboard and dragged him to the shore.

Sometimes, fights would break out when the crew had enjoyed one too many in their favourite drinking haunt. Bamse would intervene by jumping up and, with his paws on their shoulders, gentle separate the opponents.

This extraordinary dog even hopped on the local bus to Dundee when he knew members of the crew were had gone to the Bodega Bar there. He knew exactly where it was and would round up the crew and herd them back to the bus and escort them to the ship.

As his deeds became more widely known, Bamse was adopted as the mascot of the Royal Norwegian Navy and later as mascot of all Norwegian Free Forces.

He died of a heart attack in Montrose in 1944 and was buried with full military honours. More than 800 Norwegian sailors and free forces, allied soldiers and sailors and residents of Montrose attended the funeral.

Later, The People's Dispensary for Sick Animals (PDSA) awarded Bamse their Gold Medal, which is considered equivalent to the George Medal for bravery and dedication to duty. He is the only Norwegian dog to receive the award.

After the funeral, a statue of Bamse was erected in Montrose and this caught the attention of the Norwegians in Honningsvåg, Bamse's former home. A fund-raising campaign was initiated and the Minister of Defence in Norway agreed to pay NOK 70,000 (in today's money, the equivalent of £6,289 ($8,084, €7,172) towards purchasing and installing the duplicate bronze statue you see today in Honningsvåg.

It has been noted that the statue of Bamse in Montrose looks northeast towards northern Norway – and the duplicate statue in Honningsvåg similarly looks southwest to Montrose.

Bamse's statue in *Holmen* stands immediately outside the **Nordkappmuseet (North Cape Museum)**, which tells Bamse's story in detail.

The museum attracts about 10,000 visitors a year and highlights the coastal culture and fisheries industry in the region. It presents at least five different exhibitions and also covers the North Cape region

The museum is open every day between 10am and 4pm every day between 16th June and 16th September.

A couple of minutes' walk away is the *Artico Ice Bar*, which like other ice bars is reconstructed each year, using 55 blocks of ice weighing 800 kilos (0.78 Imp. Tons) and 4,200 LED lamps.

A light, sound and multi-media show transports visitors into the arctic world of northern Norway, the midnight sun and aurora.

The bar is open whenever a cruise ship is in port and stays open until it leaves. The entry fee is NOK 149 (£13.39, $17, 21, €15.27) and includes thermal clothing and two non-alcoholic drinks in ice glasses. There is also a shop with a wide selection of items representing local fauna, books, silver craft, Nordic design, warm clothes, pictures and postcards etc., as well a wide range of Christmas decorations from Scandinavian suppliers.

Many of the delights of Honningsvåg are free – not least wandering along the quayside by the small boat marina and fish processing sheds.

Summer is a very special time for the inhabitants of Honningsvåg, not least because of the winter weather and summer storms.

Sunny days and strolling among the wooden clapboard buildings reveal some fascinating surprises – red and yellow poppies growing wild by the roadside and windowsills imaginatively adorned with flowers.

For visitors who like to include a little culture in their itinerary, the ***Perleporten Kulturhus (House of Culture/North Cape Cafe Theatre)*** at Storgatan 19 is the answer.

Quite apart from offering much acclaimed cake and waffles, this group of local actors put on a lively 45-minute musical show (in English) with catchy music, song, dance, monologues and hilarious jokes to give an

insight into the challenges and rewards of what they entitle 'Our Northernmost Life'.

The show is at 1pm and highly recommended. Ticket price varies but is usually NOK 250 (£22.50, $28.86, €25.60), which given the rave reviews by many cruise passengers is worth every penny.

Perhaps one aspect of the 'northernmost life' is the need to escape the weather in a warm and cosy pub. There is such a pub just up the road from the *Kulturhuset* at Larsjorda No. 1. It is, perhaps aptly,

called **Nøden,** which means *The Need* or *The Emergency.*

The pub is more of a local haunt than a tourist attraction, but if you happen to be a Manchester United fan, this is the pub to visit; the local Manchester United Supporters Club meets here for every televised game.

Unfortunately, the pub is open only in the evenings, but if your ship is overnighting in Honningsvåg and you feel the need...

If you have been to the North Cape previously and are spending your day in Honningsvåg just enjoying the town and the scenery, the church is also worth a visit.

Consecrated in 1885 after a hurricane demolished the old church, this is the oldest building in Honningsvåg. Every single building except the church and the morgue was razed to the ground in the autumn of 1944 by retreating German troops.

When they had left, almost the entire population was evacuated to southern Norway. The first to return in the summer of 1945 found nothing but wreckage – and a gleaming, whitewashed church that was still intact.

It was the only place where they could shelter from the weather, sleep and eat. People slept on the pews, in and under the pulpit, in the tower and gallery and even by the altar.

They set up a kitchen and a bakery where they made enough bread for 100 people every day. Eventually, they built communal housing and by the end of 1945, the church was finally restored to its original purpose.

Finally, why not treat yourself to

lunch at the *King Crab Restaurant* on Sjøgata?

Awarded a Certificate of Excellence in 2017-2018, this fully licensed restaurant serves seafood and Norwegian-Scandinavian cuisines.

The bar/coffee house/restaurant is on the waterfront close to the cruise ships enclosure and offers free Wi-Fi. According to some passengers, it has the best crab soup they have ever tasted and, as the establishment's name suggests, substantial plates of King Crab!

***

KIRKENES

Kirkenes is very much a frontier town. Unprepossessing. It is located 250-miles (400-kilometres) north of the Arctic Circle, it is the easternmost (as opposed to northernmost) town in Norway and if you were to travel due south, you would end up east of St. Petersburg, Istanbul and Alexandria in Egypt.

The Russian border at Storskog, (meaning 'Big Forest) is 10 miles (16 kilometres) away and if it is not a ship's excursion, it can be reached by riverboat or the No. 901 bus from the Scandic Hotel.

With the border so close, it is not surprising that  about ten per cent of the 3,529 population are Russians or that Russian influence is everywhere. Street and other signs are in two languages and Russian is spoken widely. A Russian market comes to town each month.

As with most Norwegian towns in the north, winter activities include dog-sledding, snowmobile tours, Northern Lights, ice fishing and King Crab safaris.

In summer, the main attractions are a bus or riverboat trip to the Russian border, quad bike safaris, hiking and bird watching in the countryside.

Ships tours to the border usually also take in a small Skolt Sami encampment about which there is an aura of sadness. There are only about 400 Skolt Sami left now, mostly based around Inari in Finland.

The Skolts originally resided in the area covering northeastern Norway, North Finland and Western Russia, but when the national borders of these countries were drawn up in the 19th century, the people were divided and were subsequently victims of wars, revolutions and repression.

At the Skolt camp at Sandnes, near Kirkenes, a handful of Skolt will sing Sami songs, show off their

colourful clothing and a cradle made of reindeer hide. Visitors may also sample reindeer bouillon, which is delicious.

There are no reindeer at the encampment, but there is certainly evidence of them in the countryside nearby. This is really the beginning of the Russian *taiga* and the area around Kirkenes is also home to lynx, wolves, brown bears, elk and moose.

Sadly, with so few Skolt left, they face many tough challenges and their future is uncertain.

When, in 1906, a mining company discovered rich iron ore seams in the county of Sydvaranger, just north of Kirkenes, it provided jobs and a thriving economy in the region until the mine closed in 1996 due to bankruptcy caused in turn by low efficiency and depressed prices.

Kirkenes was immediately transformed from a mining town to a town with a mine as tourism and boom-and-bust businesses became ascendant.

An Australian mining company, Northern Iron Ltd, took over the mine and re-opened it in 2009, but was subsequently criticised for polluting the fjord and giving nothing back to the community. The company subsequently went bust and the mine was closed once again with the loss of 400 jobs.

Since then, prices doubled and an American company, Orion Mine Finance, is reported to have provided $20 million working capital to re-open the mines and is said to be ready to invest $200 million once the mining operations begin.

The Norwegian-Russian border

The only place you can cross into Russia from Norway (and vice versa) is at ***Storskog Frontier Post.*** Visitors are advised that photography is permitted but not of any Russian military installations or personnel, which pretty much rules out the point of going there., especially as there is almost nothing else to see.

In 1940, Kirkenes was occupied by German forces and a year later, the country of Sydvaranger in which Kirkenes lies became the staging area for the German offensive on the Soviet Union.

However, the assault ground to a halt and little, if any, progress was made for three years. During that time, Soviet forces bombed Kirkenes, which the Germans were using as a naval base, almost continuously.

Only Malta suffered more bombing raids and Kirkenes was eventually almost totally destroyed. All in all, it suffered 320 air attacks and the sirens were sounded more than 1,000 times. On 4th July, 1944 no fewer than 140 houses were left in flames.

Most of the population sought shelter in the *Andersgrotta*, a vast underground air raid bunker in the town centre.

The Germans had amassed some 200,000 troops on what became known as the Murmansk Front (Murmansk being the stated objective of the German offensive) with almost half of them billeted in Kirkenes.

In military actions, some 65,000 Soviet troops were captured and interned in appalling conditions in some 60 separate camps.

During the latter stages of the war, Finland withdrew from its alliance with Germany and the Germans began to retreat, torching the few remaining buildings in Kirkenes as the Red Army advanced.

Many residents of the town fled to the countryside, living in the forest and digging shelters in the hillsides. They had almost no food and suffered dreadfully. One family escaped across a fjord in a rowing boat with a Russian plane, whose pilot took them for Germans, in pursuit.

Eventually, the Russian army liberated the remains of Kirkenes, which was almost totally destroyed. Only 13 houses were left standing in a town that had been home to some 4,000 people at the time.

The Germans even blew up their own food stores to prevent the Russian troops finding them and mined all the roads to slow down the Russian advance. Meanwhile, they forced most of the population to evacuate the town and retreat with them.

Food was a major problem for the few people who were able to remain in Kirkenes. With no food stores left, no shops and no supply lines, they were faced with mass starvation. As the survivors returned from the hills and forests, they gave the Russians a huge welcome and

The Russians gave them food, albeit initially only hunks of bread and some butter.

Andersgrotta **(Anders' Shelter)** is open for groups of 10 or more people but tours must be booked 24 hours in advance at either the Scandic Hotel or Thon Hotel. The tour includes a 10-minute film about Kirkenes and what life was like for civilians there during the war. The commentary is in English, German and Norwegian and the entrance fee is NOK 200 (£18.10, $23.15, €28.50).

The Russian troops who liberated Kirkenes are remembered now with the *Soviet Liberation Monument* on Roald Amundsen's Gate.

The *Grenselandmuseet (Borderland Museum)* on Foerstevannslia, at the southern end of Kirkenes gives a detailed explanation of the war years and focusses on how people managed during the constant bombardments and food shortages.

The museum reveals some surprising facts, such as the young men of Kirkenes who joined the Red Army. These partisans escaped from the Germans and ended up on the Kola Peninsula in Russia, where they were trained as spies. They then returned to the coast to observe German ship movements and military activity and report back to the Soviets.

After the war, the Soviet Union was no longer an ally and during the Cold War, the partisans were sadly vilified as being communist sympathisers.

A Soviet Ilyushin IL2 aircraft on display was retrieved from a lake nearby where it crashed and sank, killing the rear gunner. The pilot escaped and made it back to the Soviet Union.

After retrieving the aircraft, the Norwegians gave it back to the Soviets, who returned it as a gift when the Borderland Museum opened.

Another touching exhibit is a blanket belonging to the wife of one of the partisans who was captured and executed. The Germans sent his wife, Dagny, to several camps in both Germany and Poland, and she took with her the blanket now on display. Each time the Germans moved her, she embroidered the name of the camp on the blanket and eventually donated it to the Borderland Museum.

The museum also showcases the iron ore mines at Bjørnevatn port near Kirkenes. As many as 3,000 Kirkenes residents fled to the mines and lived in them for several months. Eleven women gave birth in the tunnels.

What makes the Borderland Museum so different from other war museums is that it spotlights the stories of the people involved, rather than merely housing displays of uniforms, guns and the detritus of war.

For that reason, this museum is highly recommended. And as one reviewer observed: 'Let's face it, there is not much to do in Kirkenes so you will probably end up there anyway'.

The museum is a 20-minute walk from the centre of Kirkenes and is open between 10am and 2pm in the winter months and 10am to 6pm in the summer. The entrance fee is an extremely reasonable NOK 40 (£3.60, £4.60, €4.10), reduced from NOK 50.

Sharing the same building is the *Savio Museum* dedicated to the internationally renowned Sami artist, John Savio.

An abundance of his woodcuts, watercolours and

sketches are on display, the bold woodcuts reflecting Sami life, reindeer, wolves, dogs and the Nature of Lapland being his most prolific output.

Born in 1902, he was especially inspired by Edvard Munch, Dürer and Japanese art. Racked by tuberculosis and poverty, he died aged 36 having avoided the art world establishment and remained true to his own uniqueness.

Today, he is seen as an exceptional artist who possessed an extraordinary ability to express emotion and reflect through the strength and simplicity of his work the inner meaning of life in the North.

His is a wonderful exhibition and well worth the walk to the Borderland Museum of which it is a part.

***

EPILOGUE

Kirkenes is the furthest port of call for the Hurtigruten ships which sail to ports along the entire Norwegian coast each day, so it seems fitting to bring *The Ultimate Cruise Passenger's Guide to Norway* to an end here, too.

This book is not intended to be exhaustive, merely as the title suggests a guide to Norway and the main ports of call from a personal perspective.

I have not included some of the smaller cruise destinations – Eidsvoll, Ulsteinsvik and so on – because they are too similar to other destinations with, perhaps, not quite so much to offer in terms of attractions.

This is not to say that they are in any way less worthy of a visit and passengers who do find themselves in these towns and villages will undoubtedly be able to enjoy the wonderful nature that envelops them.

In Spring, the wild flowers in Norway always bloom. The air is always clean and fresh. The fjords, the ocean and countless islands and skerries are eternally mysterious and riveting. When the sea reflects the midnight sun on a calm evening, it transforms the surface into liquid gold.

In winter, Atlantic storms batter the coastal towns and villages, but the mountains usually are capped with snow and it is these elements that bestow this country with such beauty and which in turn are its real attractions.

It is these things that, with justification, have earned the voyage north along the Norwegian coast the reputation for being the most beautiful voyage in the world.

SH.